FRONTIERS OF
CRIMINOLOGY

FRONTIERS OF CRIMINOLOGY

Summary of the Proceedings of the
BRITISH CONGRESS ON CRIME
5–9 September 1966
University College, London

Edited by
HUGH J. KLARE
Secretary, Howard League for Penal Reform

and

DAVID HAXBY
General Secretary,
National Association of Probation Officers

HV6947
.B67
1966

Introduced by
T. C. N. GIBBENS
Reader in Forensic Psychiatry,
University of London

82865

PERGAMON PRESS
OXFORD · LONDON · EDINBURGH · NEW YORK
TORONTO · SYDNEY · PARIS · BRAUNSCHWEIG

Pergamon Press Ltd., Headington Hill Hall, Oxford
4 & 5 Fitzroy Square, London W.1
Pergamon Press (Scotland) Ltd., 2 & 3 Teviot Place, Edinburgh 1
Pergamon Press Inc., 44–01 21st Street, Long Island City, New York 11101
Pergamon of Canada, Ltd., 6 Adelaide Street East, Toronto, Ontario
Pergamon Press (Aust.) Pty. Ltd., 20–22 Margaret Street, Sydney, N.S.W.
Pergamon Press S.A.R.L., 24 rue des Écoles, Paris 5e
Vieweg & Sohn GmbH, Burgplatz 1, Braunschweig

First edition 1967

Library of Congress Catalog Card No. 66/23048

Printed in Great Britain by Cox & Wyman Ltd.,
London, Reading and Fakenham
2551/67

CONTENTS

EDITOR'S NOTE

THIS book attempts to provide a record of the Proceedings of the British Congress on Crime. It would have been impossible to publish in full all the papers delivered at the Congress, and the task we set ourselves was to produce a text reflecting the subjects discussed at the Congress and providing a survey of current thinking about crime and delinquency in so far as it was represented at the Congress.

Three Keynote Lectures were delivered to plenary sessions of the Congress, forming focal points around which other papers could be grouped. These lectures are here reproduced in full. The remaining text is based on summaries provided by the speakers, with additional notes from rapporteurs. The papers are not referred to in the order in which they appeared on the programme, but have been grouped to provide some continuity of sense and to relate them to the framework provided by the Keynote Lectures.

Unfortunately, two speakers, noted in Appendix B, were unable to supply summaries, and reference to their papers had to be omitted from the text. For the remainder, we have tried to convey accurately the findings and thoughts of the speakers, but it has sometimes been necessary to abbreviate what was supplied to us, or to expand this by reference to the original paper; and we have occasionally added links or observations of our own.

The references appended to the Keynote Lectures were supplied by the authors of those sections. In the remainder of the book we have not attempted to give detailed references but have tried to leave the text unencumbered by incorporating essential references as they occurred.

We wish to make it clear that the views expressed are those of the experts addressing the Congress, and do not necessarily reflect our own.

We would like to express our thanks to Mr. Iain Scarlet for his help with the preparation of the manuscript.

H.J.K.
D.A.H.

INTRODUCTION

WHEN planning of the first British Congress on Crime began, the members of the organizing committee, under the chairmanship of Hugh Klare, set themselves a number of objectives. The first was to see that the participants were not limited to "criminologists". Those engaged in research and teaching in the main branches of criminology in England are a small and friendly group who meet one another quite often to report progress in their work. But one of the main underlying ideas of the Congress was to invite the participation of a much wider range of people who are only marginally concerned with criminal behaviour. Although, as Hall-Williams has said, "criminologists should not stray too far from the consideration of behaviour legally defined as criminal", it is clear that the penal system is the last resort for a whole range of behaviour disorders which are, or could be, very largely dealt with by other means of social control. Perhaps the most important characteristic of the penal system—and certainly the source of its main difficulties—is that it never refuses a customer. Schoolmasters exclude children from school; mental hospitals refuse patients; alcoholics, drug addicts and vagrants are turned away by many social agencies; but the prisons never turn anyone away.

Yet those of us who work near or in the penal system are liable to become institutionalized, like the inmates. Traditional methods of dealing with problems easily become accepted as inevitable. One-third of boys in approved schools, as Asuni has shown, cannot be distinguished in any important clinical respect from one-third of those in schools for the educationally maladjusted; their different location may largely depend upon the particular administrative wheels which first started turning. Or again, many hundreds of offenders are remanded in custody for a medical report, although, as West has shown, only a minority are homeless, had previous convictions, are violent or dangerous, or have other characteristics which would rule out the possibility of obtaining a medical report on bail. Yet here, too, the Prison Medical Service never refuses to make a report in two or three weeks, and does not maintain, like Health Service clinics, that there are no vacant appointments for a month or more. The Criminal Justice Bill seeks to deal with a number of these problems.

It is not only a question of the smooth and efficient organization of services for recognized situations. Society's definitions of crime are constantly changing. New offences are being defined, such as possession of newly forbidden drugs; while there are many ways of conducting company business, such as Mr. Finer showed, which are not illegal although the majority of citizens might be inclined to define them as fraudulent.

Considerations of this kind persuaded the organizers to plan a conference which would consider the social context of crime, and to invite a wide range of participants. Social workers, schoolmasters, children's officers, doctors and lawyers, who are not primarily concerned with crime or delinquency, were invited to talk about their work so that the criminal aspects could be seen in a wider perspective.

The second principle was to eschew any attempt to cover the whole field of crime, but to single out those aspects of criminal or deviant behaviour which had been the subject of new research. Excessive generalization is one of the bugbears of criminology and it was thought better to consider limited topics in a fair degree of depth. White-collar crime and the definition of company fraud have little in common with the motoring recidivist, the drug addict or violent sex offender.

The hope was that information about the research methods as well as the research results of experts outside the field of criminology would provide useful cross-fertilization. There were many instances in which this hope was realized. The question of "typologies", for example, is a very general one in all the behavioural sciences. Research into the comparative effectiveness of different methods of penal treatment will make little progress until valid and reliable methods of classifying the many types of offender have been evolved. Yet there is much in common between classifying alcoholics and probationers, offending motorists and some kinds of mental patient; methods of assessing the interaction of therapist and client are applicable to many disciplines. There are also many comparable problems in establishing criteria of success in treatment, whether psychiatric or penal. One can choose objective criteria of relapse or re-conviction but it may be very important to consider long- and short-term effects and changes of state in personal and social adjustment in other respects.

The reader will be able to judge from the following papers and summaries whether these objectives were achieved. But it may be salutary to consider where the first Congress failed and what improvements would be needed if a second Congress were organized in a few years' time. The most outstanding deficiencies can perhaps be blamed on the present state of criminology itself. The Congress welcomed the participation of some judges and several members of police forces, two groups who are often absent from criminological meetings. But what would a judge have taken away from the conference with regard to any really valid information about the results of treatment or about sentencing policy? Unfortunately, very little. And what could any police officer have learned about the techniques of committing crime, of the means of communication between offenders, the frequency or psychology of the professional criminal? Equally little. Until much more is spent on criminological research and the training of competent workers, progress will be slow and the practitioners will wait in vain for their answers. Little was said about the relative expenditures upon services and research into their effectiveness, or how the penal system stands in this respect in comparison with the Health, Education, and Social Services.

Perhaps the most striking absentee from the conference, and one usually left out of the discussion, was the general public. Public attitudes play a large part in all the public services, but it is especially in relation to crime that so much is decided in the name of public opinion. The Criminal Law rests, we are told, upon the consensus of public opinion. Yet estimates of this public opinion seem to depend all too often on a few letters to the Press. The Congress was not able to produce any information on this topic. The limited studies which have been made seem to suggest that the "common man's" attitude to many indictable offences is not very different from the middle-class motorist's view of the 30 mile an hour speed limit, that there is a double standard, on the one hand of generally recognized behaviour involving a certain amount of illegal behaviour, and another standard involving a rather grudging consent to the provisions of the Criminal Law. Those who get caught deserve what they get, but this does not imply that their behaviour is particularly irresponsible or unusual. Perhaps, even in an egalitarian democracy such as ours, the law is more often a question of the ruling classes (whether pop singers, bishops, industrialists, trade union leaders, or cabinet ministers) imposing their views on the ruled than is commonly believed. Such questions lie at the heart of the problem of social control of deviant behaviour, and lack of information about the consumer leaves a large gap. If a second conference is planned in a few years' time perhaps these deficiencies may be made up.

The organizing committee owes a great debt to its Chairman, Hugh Klare, whose own personal initiative was largely responsible for launching and organizing the Congress. We were also most grateful to Lord Stonham, Parliamentary Under Secretary of State at the Home Office, for his encouragement and for consenting to open it.

T.C.N.G.

FIRST KEYNOTE LECTURE

I

A CENTURY OF CAUSAL THEORY

NIGEL WALKER (XXVI)

The question which this paper is intended to answer is "What stage
has been reached in the development of criminological explanations
during the last century?" To handle such an elephantine topic within
a limited space calls for unusual tactics. Instead of tracing the rise
and fall of theoretical empires in chronological order (a task which
has already been achieved by Professor Vold[1] and more recently
Professor Radzinowicz,[2]), I shall try to approach what is—or ought
to be—our present position by a logical route. The landmarks along
this route, when closely examined, turn out to consist mainly of
abandoned assumptions, and by considering these briefly we may
learn something about the road ahead.

THE CONTENT OF CAUSAL THEORY

Some of these abandoned assumptions are formal; that is they are
assumptions about the form which the explanation of criminal or
anti-social behaviour should take. These will be dealt with in the next
section. For the moment I am concerned with assumptions about the
content of criminological explanation; that is about the sort of things
which criminologists have regarded as "causes" of crime.

When theological and philosophical speculation about crime began
to give place to scientific reasoning, two rival assumptions led social
scientists in different directions. To Quetelet in Belgium, Guerry in
France and Porter in England crime was a symptom of an unhealthy
society. To Morel, Lombroso and Maudsley (all, by the way, psychiatrists) it was the symptom of an abnormal individual. The sociologists saw the "dangerous and criminal classes" as the product of
rapidly growing towns. The "noble savages" of eighteenth-century
poets and philosophers had become Victor Hugo's "savages of

3

civilization". To Morel, on the other hand, criminality was one symptom of the "degeneracy" which he also detected in epileptics, lunatics and mental defectives. Morel, by the way, seems to me to deserve the title of "Founder of the Biological School" rather than Lombroso. But it is the latter who figures in the history books because he had at least one advantage over Morel: he had read and accepted Darwin and could therefore explain Morel's degeneracy as "atavism"—a step backward in the evolutionary process.

The sociological and individualistic approaches, however, had at least one feature in common, which can fairly be called "the assumption of pathology". Crime was for both of them a sign that something had gone wrong. In the event, it was a sociologist who first questioned the assumption. Durkheim's main contribution to modern sociological criminology was no doubt the concept of "anomie"; but there is a danger of overlooking the importance of his chapter on "The Normal and the Pathological" in *The Rules of Sociological Method*,[3] where he argues that

> ... crime itself plays a useful role in this evolution [*sc.* of society]. Crime implies not only that the way remains open to necessary changes but that in certain cases it directly prepares these changes. Where crime exists, collective sentiments are sufficiently flexible to take on a new form, and crime sometimes helps to determine the form they will take. How many times, indeed, it is only an anticipation of future morality—a step toward what will be!

This was, of course, an overstatement, which committed the usual mistake of discussing crime as if it were a homogeneous phenomenon. But whether or not crime was essential to progress, overstatement certainly was.

The individualists have been slower than the sociologists to modify the assumption of pathology. By the twentieth century they were clearly divided into biological individualists—the intellectual descendants of Morel and Lombroso—and psychological individualists who drew their inspiration from Binet and later from Freud and Pavlov. The biological school regarded criminals as genetic casualties (a point of view which still derives some support from twin studies) and continued to do so until Sheldon turned their thoughts in a new direction by developing Kretschmer's theory of the relationship between body-build and mental illness into an explanation of normal variations in personality. In his somatotypology criminals were no longer degenerates or atavisms, but merely mesomorphs. If Sheldon, by the way, had read less of Kretschmer and more of Darwin, it might have occurred to him that this, too, could be explained in terms of natural selection, or—more precisely—natural self-selection. Sturdy athletic little mesomorphs are more likely than asthenic ectomorphs (or heavy endomorphs) to find fighting or running away from police and shopkeepers a rewarding activity.

Psychological individualists were also slow to modify the assumption of pathology. It is true that one of the most important features of the Freudian revolution was the implication that normal human beings were born without morals and had to acquire them. But so powerful was the traditional notion of man's original innocence that even Freud's most devoted followers continued to regard delinquents as people who would have been moral had they not been damaged by some traumatic event or compelled by some unconscious need. Just as theologians believed that everyone must have a conscience, so the first generations of Freudians, with their highly respectable European upbringing, assumed that everyone must have a super-ego. Anthropologists such as Malinowski could have contradicted them, but did not: it was not until the 1930's and 1940's that they began to relate cultures and types of personality and to realize that in some societies the fuel of morality is not guilt but shame—not self-condemnation but fear of condemnation by others. As for the possibility that even in "guilt societies" children could grow up without acquiring a capacity for feeling guilt, this was not fully accepted until anthropologists began to explore the wilds of Paddington and Brooklyn as well as New Mexico and the Pacific.

On the whole, however, Pavlov's descendants have been readier than Freud's to accept and develop the notion that innocence is something which is learned, not lost; that if man is outside Eden it is not because he was expelled but because he failed to qualify for entry. The application of Pavlov's ideas to delinquency has been due largely to the work of Mowrer and Eysenck, but the most sophisticated exposition of this approach is that of Trasler.[4]

Recent estimates of the prevalence of delinquency—for instance among Stockholm schoolchildren—have cast still more doubt on the assumption of pathology. The larger the percentage of a population or age group which seems to indulge in occasional dishonesty the less realistic is it to regard this percentage as pathological or even eccentric. Indeed, the question at the moment is whether there are not areas and age groups in which a clear conscience is abnormal (note that I do not say "pathological"). I am far from arguing that

B

no kinds of crime can safely be regarded as abnormal in themselves and pathological in origin; or that repeated and persistent dishonesty is common enough to be accepted as normal in any area or age group. What I am contending is that what are abnormal and pathological are some rather special subgroups of what appears in the criminal statistics.

FORMAL ASSUMPTIONS

Other abandoned assumptions are *formal:* that is, they are assumptions about the form which the explanation of criminal or anti-social behaviour is likely to take.

Monoliths

An obvious example was the monolithic assumption that it would be possible to define the cause in terms of a single concept. Tudor legislators were concerned about "idleness, mother and root of all vices, whereby hath insurged and sprung . . . continual thefts, murders and other heinous offences and great enormities" (the statute of 22, Henry VIII, c. 12). A nineteenth-century example, Morel's "degeneracy" and its Lombrosian descendant, has already been mentioned.

Twentieth-century monoliths are slightly more elaborate. It has been the fate of most great social scientists to inspire over-enthusiastic generalizations by their followers. Binet, by developing intelligence tests, inadvertently encouraged the belief that criminals were of low intelligence. An *obiter dictum* of Freud's about *some* criminals was inflated into the statement that "the unconscious need for punishment . . . is the key to all problems of delinquency".[5] Less specific but correspondingly more plausible is the assumption that all delinquents are mentally disordered, or at best "maladjusted". (Strictly speaking this belongs to the seventeenth rather than the twentieth century, for even Hale wrote: "Doubtless most persons that are felons . . . are under a degree of partial insanity when they commit these offences".[6])

The increasing use of the criminal law for administrative purposes, such as the collection of revenue and the control of disease or motor-cars, made it implausible to regard everyone who appeared in the criminal courts as degenerate, feeble-minded, maladjusted or insecure. But even sociologists, who must have realized this, have been unable to rid themselves of a tendency to erect and worship mono-liths. Tarde's laws of imitation inspired Sutherland's theory of differential association; and Wilkins's "general theory of deviance" is yet another attempt to use the concept of communication in a way that is more sophisticated than Tarde's or Sutherland's, but no less monolithic.

Sociologists who are sophisticated enough to confine their hypo-theses to a few legal subdivisions of criminal behaviour are often none the less monolithic in their approach. Cressey explained all "trust violation" as something which "takes place when the position of trust is viewed by the trusted person according to culturally provided knowledge about and rationalizations for using the en-trusted funds for solving a non-shareable problem".[7] He boldly con-tinued: "Whenever the conjuncture of events occurs, trust violation results, and if the conjunction does not take place there is no trust violation", although if he had been able to investigate cases in which employees had been tempted to embezzle but had refrained he would probably have found that they included cases in which his necessary and sufficient condition was also fulfilled. This intermediate stage, in which we have several monoliths for several legal subdivisions of crime, might appropriately be called the "Stonehenge Era" of criminology.

Multiple Determination

The assumption which has gradually been replacing the monolithic approach is attributable to Burt in England and Healey in the U.S.A. Burt called it "the fact of multiple determination"[8] by which he meant that in the case of many individual delinquents it was necessary to assume that there were at least two (and often nine or ten) "sub-versive circumstances" which "conspired" to produce the delinquent behaviour. In less metaphorical language, whereas the monolithic approach looked only for the single variable whose value differed markedly from normal, Healey and Burt looked for two or more such variables. Moreover, it was not necessary that any of these variables should have a *markedly* abnormal value; slight variations in the wrong direction in several variables (none of which need by themselves be remarkable) could produce delinquency.

The number of causal investigations by criminologists which genuinely apply the assumption of multiple determination, as distinct from the assumption of a choice of monoliths is not as large as might be supposed. Burt's own was an example. Others are Ferguson's study of a school-leaving cohort of 1349 Glasgow boys[9] which is described in *The Young Delinquent in his Social Setting*, and the Gluecks' most recent analysis of the data from their comparison of 500 delinquent and 500 non-delinquent Massachusetts boys[10] (in *Family Environment and Delinquency*). The logical form of the sort of conclusions to which this approach leads is illustrated by the Gluecks' statement that ". . . paternal drunkenness is likely to convert the trait of *introversiveness*, which normally is no more characteristic of delinquents than of non-delinquents, into one directed towards anti-social purposes."*

Here two factors, neither necessarily sufficient by themselves to produce delinquency, are said to have this result when they combine.

This approach has been attacked by Cohen and more recently by Wilkins (whose monolithic general theory of deviance has already been mentioned) on the grounds that "it does not facilitate the deduction of any hypotheses or practical consequences that are of any help whatsoever" and ". . . is framed in such a way that it is impossible to find any test whereby it could be proved wrong". It is, he argues, "an anti-theory which proposes that no theory can be formed regarding crime".[11] This is the debater's trick of assigning his opponent a role which the latter never meant to fill, and then pointing out that he is not playing it properly. The assumption of multiple determination is neither a theory nor an anti-theory, but an hypothesis about theories. It suggests that nothing which can be regarded as a single variable will ever be found to explain, without exceptions, any group of delinquents or delinquent acts; and that only a theory formulated in terms of two or more variables has any prospect of doing so. Contrary to Wilkins's assertion, it is not untestable:† it is tested every time a new monolith is erected and demolished. Nor is it as unhelpful as Wilkins suggests; for it warns us not to waste our time in erecting monoliths.

---

* I am, of course, citing this as an example of the *form* which a causal statement can take, not as an instance of a particularly successful explanation.

† Except in the sense that no statement of the form "no X will ever be found to be Y" is completely verifiable.

The Dangers of Measurement

Nevertheless the new approach creates new dangers and enhances old ones. Especially enhanced are the dangers that surround the measurement of possibly relevant factors. When investigators cease to ask questions of the form "Is factor X present or not?" (e.g. "Is this home stable or not?") and substitute questions of the form "What value is to be assigned to X?" (e.g. "How stable is this home?") the importance of small differences increases, and with it the influence of impressionistic assessments. This influence is increased when the investigators know whether the case they are classifying is a delinquent or control case, and when they have preconceived assumptions about the sort of factors which are associated with delinquency: both circumstances which it is almost impossible to avoid. The natural reaction to these dangers is to prefer what can be measured objectively: more precisely, to concentrate on the measurement of variables whose assessments by different judges show the fewest discrepancies. Instead of asking themselves "Shall I classify this home as 'very stable', 'stable', 'slightly unstable' or 'very unstable'?", field-workers are instructed, say, to record the number of absences of either parent for more than X weeks during the last Y years. As this example illustrates, the more objectively the variable can be quantified, the less likely is it to be what the investigator really wants to measure. At best it will be a variable which is known to be highly correlated with what he wants to measure: but more often the correlation must simply be assumed.

The Assumption of Constancy

Another assumption which most investigators are forced to make is that the variables which they have decided to measure are more or less constant, so that they can all be measured at any convenient time. Thus if the investigators are interested in the interaction between paternal discipline and the son's intelligence (to take another example from the Gluecks) they are more or less forced to assume that the son has always been (say) above average in intelligence and that father always disciplined him in much the same way. In the case of intelligence this is a plausible assumption; in the case of parental discipline it is less so. Parents change (for the worse or the better) in the course of their child-rearing; and the last born may be treated very differently from the first-born (especially if the first-born has dis-graced the family). Obvious as the point seems, it needed Dr. Gibbens[12] to remind us of it.

The point can be made in a more extreme form. It is not merely that some of the relevant factors are things of the past, no longer observable. What distinguishes *some* delinquents from non-delinquents may be a *sequence* of events, none of them simultaneous and none of them peculiar to delinquents. An analogy from car-driving will illustrate the point. Two drivers may drive similar cars at similar speeds over the same stretch of road with similar numbers of vehicles passing them and pedestrians crossing in front of them, but a certain sequence of such events may cause one of them to have an accident while the other does not. There are obvious and important dif-ferences between having an accident and committing an intentional crime. But let us imagine two brothers, one 3 years older than the other, growing up in a reasonably stable and harmonious home. When the older one is 5 years old, his father is placed under stress by some outside circumstance, such as uncertainty about the future of his job, and behaves ill-temperedly to his family. The younger son, being still a baby, is not affected, but the 4-year-old is. By the time the younger boy is of an age to be affected by his father's moods, these have improved. Later, the older boy finds him-self in a school class with an ill-tempered master, and is provoked into some act of hostility, which is labelled "malicious damage". May I, for the sake of brevity, label such cases "fortuitous" delinquents?

A similar point has been made by Howard Becker in his book about marihuana users:

> We need, for example, one kind of explanation of how a person comes to be in a situation where marihuana is easily available to him, and another kind of explanation of why, given the fact of its availability, he is willing to ex-periment with it in the first place. And we need still another explanation of why, having experience with it, he continues to use it. In a sense each explanation constitutes a necessary cause of the behaviour. ... Yet the variables which account for each may not, taken separately, distinguish between users and non-users. ... .[13]

If such cases occur in more than negligible numbers, they will defeat investigations that proceed by analysing data collected at any single point of time, however sophisticated the techniques of analysis. Noth-ing but a cohort study of almost unimaginable thoroughness could reveal them. The only way of countering this disquieting possibility is to assume that such causal sequences are likely to be confined to cases in which the individual commits only one delinquent act, or in which his delinquencies are confined to a single short period. If so, investigations which concentrate on offenders with histories of repeated delinquencies over considerable periods could be assumed to have virtually excluded such cases. Unfortunately it is possible that the successful and undetected commission of a satisfying offence may of itself provide the offender with a motive for repeating it, so that a "fortuitous" first offender who was fortunate enough to escape detection might become a "fortuitous" recidivist. (Even eventual detection may not remedy this state of affairs if it has been preceded by enough satisfying experiences of undetected delinquency.) But these speculations (they can hardly be more) are intended only to emphasize the dangers involved in what I have called "the assumption of constancy" in the investigation of causal variables.

THE OBJECT-OF-EXPLANATION

So far I have discussed what seem to me the important assumptions which underlay or underlie criminologists' choice of explanatory factors and the form of their hypotheses. We are just beginning to realize, however, that even criminologists' notions of what they are trying to explain require examination. It is significant that we have no ready-made word or phrase for "the thing that needs explaining": (Karl Popper's attempt to import the term "explicandum"[14] has been more or less a failure). The best I can do to improvise is "object-of-explanation".

In criminology, as in other fields, there has been a difference between the object-of-explanation of the psychologist (or psychiatrist), on the one hand, and the sociologist, on the other. The psychologist —at least in the early days—was trying to explain why this or that individual committed this or that crime. The sociologist was trying to explain why "crime" (or, if he was more sophisticated, some sort of crime) was more prevalent in certain decades, cultures or districts.

The fallacy of treating "crime" in general as something to be explained in a single statement (however complex) has been obvious to criminologists since Lombroso, although this has not prevented many of them from slipping into it in unguarded moments. (Sociologists are especially prone to do so: witness the passage I quoted from Durkheim.) Less obvious, and accordingly more frequent, is the fallacy of treating legal sub-divisions of crime as if they corresponded to sub-divisions in nature. This is not completely unscientific. Two men convicted of bigamy are slightly more likely to have character-istics in common than a bigamist and a burglar. But there is a real danger in assuming that the acts comprised in one legal subdivision have more in common with each other than with acts comprised in another subdivision. Criminologists who study murders, for example, usually seem to disregard attempted murders, although the difference often depends only on chance circumstances, such as the distance to the nearest hospital. My name for this fallacy is "legal realism", because it assumes that legal names correspond to real species in nature, and are thus a sound basis for selecting the objects of criminological study.

It is possible to go further, and to question whether any clas-sification based on the criminal act is the best way of defining the object of criminological explanation. Even if we succeed in defining quite sophisticated groups of offences (such as "acts of personal violence against opposite-sexed members of the same household") so few offenders are specialists in a single sort of anti-social activity that even this is a highly artificial selection of what we want to ex-plain. It is as if ornithologists tried to explain the routes of migrants by selecting only birds who perch on telegraph poles.

Typologies

It may have been reasoning on these lines—or it may have been the nature of their own concepts—that has led psychologists to substitute another object-of-explanation—the psychological type. Crimino-logical typologies separate offenders into groups with different ab-normalities of personality, each liable to involve the individual not only in law-breaking of one sort or another, but also in disapproved behaviour that is outside the criminal law.

Typologies are unquestionably an improvement on the approach which treats the act, whether legally or otherwise defined, as the object-of-explanation. In one form or another they are as old as Lombroso's later works. Probably the best-known modern one is that of Hewitt and Jenkins,[15] whose factor-analysis of 500 child-guidance cases yielded three almost independent factors, "unsocialized aggression", "socialized delinquency" and "over-inhibition". It is unfortunate that all such investigations have begun with a biased sample of delinquents—from child-guidance clinics, short-term prisoners and so forth. But this alone does not make their findings deceptive: merely incomplete. There are certainly more delinquent types than are dreamed of in their typologies.

The sociologist, too, has refined his object-of-explanation. It is no longer the mere variation in frequency of certain prescribed acts from one period of time or one geographical area to another. It is the existence of groups of people, linked by some sort of communication —however tenuous—who seem to produce more than their share of infringements of the criminal code and other official norms of behaviour. The first such groups to be identified were the bands of vagabonds which troubled Europe in the fifteenth and sixteenth centuries; in later centuries the problem presented itself in a new form when the colonizers of Asian and African territories found unacceptable differences between their codes of behaviour and those of the indigenous populations. A later and subtler form of the phenomenon was the behaviour—real or supposed—of the immigrant groups which caused such concern in the U.S.A. early in this century. Nowadays sociologists are more interested in "gangs", "near-groups", "peer-groups" or "sub-cultures", although their definitions of these objects-of-explanation vary considerably.*

Just as some anthropologists saw connections between whole cultures and individual personality, so some sociologists have related the distribution of certain psychological types to subtler sub-cultural differences in child-rearing techniques. To this extent the psychologist's typology as an object-of-explanation is not necessarily inconsistent with the modern sociological approach. But if, like Sutherland, the sociologist wants to see how far he can get without resorting to typologies, he has his alternative. Sutherland's rather crude concept of "definitions favourable to law-breaking" has now given place to the more realistic one of "deviant norms" or "delinquent values". Sutherland seems to have pictured his criminals sitting down to discuss whether it was proper to break the law in such-and-such a way. In modern sociology they insensibly and inarticulately acquire the knowledge that such-and-such behaviour is acceptable in the circles in which they move, together with the knowledge that, for some regrettable but unexplored reason, certain forms of it happen to lead to trouble with the police.

* See Downes' recent book.[16]

Conversely, psychologists who cling to the assumption of pathology try to get along as well as they can without resorting to the hypothesis that persistent delinquency may be unconnected with psychological abnormality. But to the more open-minded psychologist—and the descendants of Pavlov seem to be more open-minded than the descendants of Freud—the deviant sub-culture is the obvious logical waste-paper basket for the occasional delinquent whom, with the best will in the world, he cannot fit into his typology. Even Hewitt and Jenkins believed in the "socialized delinquent", who was merely behaving in accordance with the norms of his peer-group, although the assumption of pathology made Hewitt and Jenkins ascribe this to parental neglect.

The sociologist's sub-culture or peer-group is just as much of a theoretical construct as the psychologist's type. ("Gangs" have stronger claims to reality, because their members will sometimes refer to themselves as members, whereas only a self-conscious intellectual admits to belonging to a sub-culture or peer-group. But gang membership in this precise sense is rare and of negligible utility to the sociologists.) Moreover, now that most psychologists no longer attempt to explain the inevitability of delinquency in this or that individual, but are content to assign him to a type which is merely very likely to behave delinquently, another logical difference between their object-of-explanation and those of the sociologist has disappeared. Just as the young male member of the Stepney sub-culture merely has a high probability and not a certainty of behaving delinquently, so those whom the psychologist assigns to the groups with "low ego-strength" or "weak super-ego" are merely likely to follow suit. Both sub-cultural theory and psychological typologies are based on probability-groups, and thus belong to what Matza[17] calls the "soft determinism" with which the social sciences must be contented.

This is not always recognized, with the result that explanatory descriptions of delinquent types or sub-cultures are sometimes said to be incomplete or defective because it is always possible to point to individuals who, though belonging to the type or sub-culture, have not in fact behaved delinquently. This sort of criticism fails to appreciate the probabilistic nature of the causal relationships described by social scientists. The only situation in which it is justified is one in which it is possible not only to point to a substantial number of "exceptions" but also to define what distinguishes them (or most of them) from the individuals who behave in accordance with the probability; in which case the critic is not demolishing the explanatory statement but refining it.

Careers

Nevertheless, both typologies and sub-cultures do entail certain dangers of over-simplification. It is only too easy to assume that all the delinquencies of the youth with a weak super-ego spring from this weakness or that all the anti-social behaviour of a delinquent sub-culture is in accordance with its norms. But the most important point which I want to make is that other kinds of objects-of-explanation may be needed if we are to progress beyond the point which we have reached. I do not mean that psychological types and sub-cultures should be *superseded*—although no doubt they will eventually be by more refined concepts which we cannot conceive at present. What I am suggesting is that even at the stage which social science has already reached they need to be *supplemented* by at least one other object-of-explanation. In addition to the type and the sub-culture we need the idea of the *career*.

The essence of this sort of object-of-explanation is that it is a sequence of events, linked by the identity of the individual concerned. It should probably include not only his anti-social actions, but also the reactions, official and unofficial, of others (and even important actions that are not inherently anti-social, such as marriage). If there is anything in this suggestion, it will eventually be possible to build up a classification of careers of different sorts. For example, a very crude classification indeed would make the following distinctions:

> Sequences which began or ended with events such as marriage, divorce, bereavement, separation from a companion, mental or physical illness.
>
> Sequences which ended with the first penal experience, or after several penal experiences, or after the first penal experience of a particular kind (such as imprisonment after a series of unsuccessful probation orders).
>
> Sequences which appear unaffected or even intensified by penal experiences.

Of course there are possibilities of misclassification, just as there are in other objects-of-explanation; but at least the data which is being grouped is more or less hard, which is more than can be said of some typologies.

Objects-of-explanation of this kind would neither commit us nor confine us to psychological or sociological explanations. Some parts of some sequences—such as a series of thefts following a bereavement—could no doubt be explained by assigning the individual to some psychologically abnormal type. But this draws attention to an advantage; it would not be *essential* to "type" him, for his reaction to the event in question might be explicable in terms of psychological processes which we regard as more or less universal. Again, some sequences—such as heavy drinking bouts after the break-up of a marriage—might be explained as culturally or sub-culturally permissible reactions. Others might call for explanations in other sociological terms, such as "roles". Obviously, too, there are sequences—such as thefts of food and clothing by absconding inmates of penal institutions—which need neither a sociologist nor a psychologist to explain them.*

Incidentally, the adoption of "the career" as an object-of-explanation would probably make it easier to draw workable distinctions between the normal and the abnormal. It is probably "normal" to commit one or two breaches of the criminal law in one's middle teens (if one is male, at least) and then to refrain from repeating them, perhaps from prudence, perhaps because one discovers other exciting diversions, perhaps—if one is unlucky—because one has actually been caught. What is "abnormal" is to persist in such behaviour, especially if one persists after being caught.

It would be ridiculous to present this suggestion as entirely new. The principle is already detectable, though not explicit, in such studies as *The Habitual Prisoner* by D. J. West[18]. On the other hand, the resemblance between my point and Howard Becker's (described in the preceding section) is only superficial, since he was arguing that some *explanations* need to be sequential in form whereas I am arguing that among the *objects-of-explanation* we need a sequential one.

THE AIM OF EXPLANATIONS

It is even possible that, as an object-of-explanation, the delinquent career will yield ideas for prevention or treatment where the concepts

---

* I have deliberately chosen crude examples because they are less likely to be controversial than subtler ones.

of the delinquent type and the delinquent sub-culture have failed to do so. (Again, I am not arguing that they should be discarded—merely supplemented.) Arguments based on profitability seem to have become more than faintly suspect, especially since criminology has become an academically respectable subject. "Surely", says the academic objector, "an explanation is something scientific, an attempt to describe the truth, which may or may not yield useful by-products such as preventive or corrective techniques, but which must not be judged by its usefulness?" But perhaps this, too, is a nineteenth-century view of social science. Must not explanations of the sort of phenomena with which we are concerned inevitably consist of selections and constructs? ("Inevitably", because anything more ambitious would not merely be hopelessly complex and incomprehensible: it would be incomplete and out-of-date by the time it had been compiled.) If so, on what principle or with what aim is the selection to be made? If the aim is explanations with the maximum universality, which apply to the greatest possible numbers of societies and eras, they will also be characterized by the maximum generality and vagueness. If the aim is the minimum number of inexplicable exceptions, they will trickle away into the sands of detail. We could well do worse than select what we have a chance of manipulating to some advantage.

If so, a closer look at the phenomena of crime from the point of view of the "career" may well direct our attention to possibilities of prevention or correction which are overlooked when one is seeing types or sub-cultures. For the prospects of modifying the norms and values of sub-cultures—especially in a society unwilling to regiment its mass media of entertainment—are obviously poor. As for the prospects of modifying psychological types, it is only in the case of the young and the mentally ill that psychologists and psychiatrists have much optimism left.

REFERENCES

1. VOLD, G. B., *Theoretical Criminology*, O.U.P., 1958.
2. RADZINOWICZ, L., *Ideology and Crime*, Heinemann, 1966.
3. DURKHEIM, E., *The Rules of Sociological Method*, 1895.
4. TRASLER, G., *The Explanation of Criminality*, Routledge & Kegan Paul, 1962.
5. GLOVER, E., *The Roots of Crime*, Imago, 1960.
6. HALE, M., *Historia Placitorum Coronae*, 1736.
7. CRESSEY, D., *Other People's Money*, Glencoe Free Press, Illinois, 1953.

8. BURT, C., *The Young Delinquent*, London University Press, 1925.
9. FERGUSON, T., *The Young Delinquent in his Social Setting*, O.U.P., 1952.
10. GLUECK, S. and E., *Family Environment and Delinquency*, 1962.
11. WILKINS, L. T., *Social Deviance*, Tavistock Publications, 1964.
12. GIBBENS, T. C. N., *Psychiatric Studies of Borstal Lads*, O.U.P., 1963.
13. BECKER, H., *The Outsiders*, Glencoe Free Press, Illinois, 1963.
14. POPPER, K., *The Poverty of Historicism*, 1957.
15. HEWITT, L. F., and JENKINS, R. L., *Fundamental Patterns of Maladjustment*, D. H. Green, Illinois, 1946.
16. DOWNES, D. M., *The Delinquent Solution*, Routledge and Kegan Paul, 1966.
17. MATZA, D., *Delinquency and Drift*, John Wiley, 1964.
18. WEST, D. J., *The Habitual Prisoner*, Macmillan, 1963.

II

SOME THEORIES ABOUT CRIME

1. ANALYTICAL THEORIES

Dr. Walker clearly feels that the assumption of "first generation Freudians" (with their highly respectable European middle-class backgrounds) that everyone, including offenders, must have a super-ego, is now *passé*. But in his paper on neurotic criminals, Dr. Hyatt Williams (XXXI) sees the matter otherwise.

It ought perhaps to be explained here that Dr. Williams is an analyst, a consultant psychotherapist who works in the Tavistock Clinic and in a London prison and therefore sees working-class offenders. He suggests a conceptual framework, based on the theories of Freud and Melanie Klein, within which, he maintains, neurotic offences take place.

At first sight, the very term "neurotic criminal" might seem contra-dictory. But it is possible to regard certain criminals as persons who have responded to internal or external stress, not by the development of neurotic symptoms or of a psychosis, but by resorting to some sort of action of a criminal kind which is performed in order to avoid stress.

There is a process of development in an individual by which an experience may first be felt in terms of persecutory anxiety. This is later digested or metabolized and finally produces a different kind of anxiety. This is not persecutory but depressive. Persecutory anxiety consists of a feeling of being got at in a damaging way by other people (or by their internalized images). Depressive anxiety is concerned with the harm which the self might do to others, especially loved ones; harm which might be done to them either actually or to their inter-nalized images. It is done with a feeling of responsibility and concern for others.

A state of persecutory anxiety stultifies and halts emotional growth whereas the capacity to face and work through depressive anxiety is the essential element in growth. By growth is meant integration and

19

maturation both within the self and in relationships to others in the family or at work. If an experience which ought to arouse depression or depressive anxiety arouses instead a strong and stronger feeling of being got at, this can reach such a pitch that something is done to disown the experience. This could be expressed as follows: D (depression)–PS (persecution)–Not-care-action to quieten or get rid of persecution–Escape from responsibility of action. If, in the process D–PS–Not-care, get rid of persecutor–Escape, no apparent conflict appears, then it might be said that the criminal is dedicated. But if many conflicts appear in the process from D–Escape, the criminal is a neurotic one.

If someone who tends to proceed from D–Escape is under inner or outer stress, there is a loss of what is called "emotional continence" and violent action can occur. This explosive behaviour occurs as the delinquent split-off part of the self breaks through. Some offenders feel preliminary anxiety. Others are as overwhelmed by a sudden catastrophe. With them there is often a denial of memory of the act— a major symptom of splitting. Anxiety may occur here as if to some other person—i.e. the part of the self which is split off.

In another group of neurotic offenders, life may have continued at an even pace for a long time since the split-off delinquent self was finding some sort of satisfaction in fantasy or in quasi-masturbatory processes. In such cases, delinquency may occur when outward circumstances suddenly appear to approximate to the inner delinquent fantasy. On such an occasion a chance person or object may take the place of the fantasy object. The crime may therefore appear to be motiveless.

A chance assault on a passer-by may take place since, in the delinquent's fantasy, the passer-by may represent a persecutor and the immediate circumstances may match the background to the persecutory fantasy. It may be also that the persecutory object is in reality a loved object—a parent, perhaps: in which case, a delinquent act cannot take place which involves that object directly. The fear of retaliation may be too great, or the fear of deprivation which would follow harming or destroying them. In such cases, a neutral object may be chosen to fulfil the conditions of the fantasy. There may be a great deal of retrospective guilt in these circumstances.

There was, for example, a youth who was carrying an axe. He was stopped by a policeman who asked him where he was going. The youth immediately attacked the policeman, inflicting severe wounds upon him. Subsequently, he wrote to the policeman from prison, apologizing to him and hoping that no serious damage was done and that the policeman would realize that there was no personal animosity felt towards him.

The criminal, Dr. William affirms, has a severe persecutory conscience, a conscience which is so strong and so savage that he is in constant rebellion against it. But in the neurotic offender conflict is always present. Detection of such a conflict might, however, be complicated by the fact that it could operate at an unconscious level. It could then only be deduced from his behaviour rather than from some overt recognition by the man in question himself.

An example of this is the need to be caught and punished when, by the use of reasonable care, the criminal could have got away with his crime. There was, for example, the man who stole a typewriter from the Inland Revenue and then took it across the road to the pub, where the Inland Revenue officials had lunch, and attempted to sell it there.

Unconscious guilt and unconscious conflict may constantly reinforce conflicts which appear to be reality ones of which the criminal is conscious. Some sort of livable balance may be achieved in which the ego is sufficiently competent to control the unconscious conflict in its conscious guise; but this may be easily upset by chance illnesses or social events. This then leads to a flare-up of anxiety and guilt which is felt to be persecutory and hence leads to further crime.

The psychotherapist welcomes the appearance of conflict since this is a useful sign for a good outcome. He deplores the ascendancy of the Mephistopholian side, with its demands for power and a cynical rejection of good values based on love and feeling for other people. If the Mephistopholian side is in the ascendancy, then the good split-off self receives little nourishment from day-to-day events and, therefore, has little opportunity for growth.

In the course of psychotherapy, the growth of love and the toleration of anxiety and pain as a natural concomitant of this has to be encouraged and accepted. The circular reinforcing mechanism of escalating delinquency has somehow to be interrupted. Thus, depression leading to feelings of persecutory anxiety, which in turn lead to delinquent acting-out, perhaps followed by momentary relief, but eventually to increasing tension and anxiety (thus contributing back to the depressive beginning of the cycle) needs somehow to be

c

interrupted by the psychotherapeutic regime. "A man by suffering shall learn, Wisdom comes against his will."

2. TYPOLOGIES

The existence of different personality types—those that lean towards depressive anxiety and those that lean towards persecutory anxiety—might go some way towards explaining why, within a high delinquency area where a good deal of delinquency proneness is manifest, there are nevertheless some who refrain from crime. In any case, it leads us to the more general question of typologies, touched upon by Dr. Walker (XXVI) and echoed in a number of group lectures.

Miss Joy Mott (XXI), of the Home Office Research Unit, comes firmly down on the side of treatment-orientated typologies. In criminological research, she maintains, the purpose of developing typological systems is to provide a tool to assist in the evaluation of the effectiveness of any single form of penal treatment as well as in the comparison of the relative effectiveness of different forms of treatment. She quotes Wilkins as suggesting

> that the outcome of treatment could be more effectively examined if an interplay is postulated between types of treatment and types of offender. The failure to note differences between treatment outcomes in the past could, by this reasoning, be due to the single form of treatment having differential effects on different types of offender.

There are two possible research approaches to the development of offender typologies. One approach would be concerned with the detailed investigation of the different treatments at present being applied followed by the subsequent classification of individual offenders in terms of their suitability for one treatment or another. The second approach would involve developing types on the basis of offender characteristics which might then yield hypotheses to assist in the planning and development of treatment strategies. This latter approach would seem, at present, the most likely to be fruitful because considerable information is already available on offender characteristics. Moreover, this second approach would not be tied to changing fashions in treatment theory and humanitarian reform.

The most important criteria for the development of offender typologies would seem to be:

(1) The inclusion of the major part of the offender population.
(2) A description of the aetiology and developmental history of each type.
(3) Indications of the behaviour to be manipulated in the treatment process.
(4) The detailed specification of the characteristics of the individual for his assignment to a given type.

Among typologies based on personality characteristics are those by Sullivan, Grant and Grant; Argyle; Scott; and Hewitt and Jenkins. Although there is little research evidence to support the validity of these typological systems there is considerable agreement between the four theorists on four varieties of offender, as follows.

(a) A type trained to anti-social standards who is thought to respond readily to re-training and who is not expected to continue offending for very long.
(b) An unsocialized or maladapted type who represents the most difficult treatment problem and who is expected to be the most persistent offender.
(c) An inadequate, immature type who is thought to "grow out" of criminal activity without the need for active treatment intervention although they may require continuous long-term support.
(d) A neurotic offender type whose criminal activities may cease or be interrupted by spontaneous remissions of the neurotic conflicts. This is the only type for whom psychotherapy is recommended.

The application to approved school boys in this country of the Hewitt and Jenkins typology is the subject of another group lecture by Miss Elizabeth Field (XI), also of the Home Office Research Unit. This typology is based on the case histories of 500 children who had attended the Michigan Child Guidance Clinic. It had led them to postulate the existence of three types of maladjustment:

(1) The unsocialized, aggression syndrome.
(2) The socialized delinquency syndrome.
(3) The over-inhibited syndrome.

Each of these behavioural syndromes was then related to a specific pattern of upbringing and the environmental influences acting upon the child were thought by Hewitt and Jenkins to determine causally the type of maladjustment shown. The environmental patterns were:

(a) The pattern of parental rejection which was related to the unsocialized, aggression syndrome.
(b) The pattern of parental negligence and exposure to delinquent behaviour which was related to the socialized delinquency syndrome.
(c) The pattern of family repression which was related to the over-inhibited syndrome.

Support for the underlying concepts of these patterns and the associations between them, in spite of considerable differences in detail, were claimed by Jenkins and Glickman (1947) when they investigated the records of 300 delinquent boys committed to the New York Training School for Boys; and by Lewis (1954) in her study of 500 children admitted to the Mersham Reception Centre, Kent. Quay (1964) investigated the case histories of 115 institutionalized male delinquents in the U.S.A. and, after a factor analysis, found four factors, three of which strongly resembled Hewitt and Jenkins behavioural syndromes.

Various objections have been made to several features in each of these studies. The Home Office study overcomes some, but not all, of these criticisms. In any case, this is the first time an attempt has been made to validate the Hewitt and Jenkins hypothesis on the basis of a wholly delinquent group in England: 274 13-year-old boys who were attending approved schools in 1962.

The same method of analysis was used. Only 39 per cent of the cases were classifiable and this coincides with the figure that Hewitt and Jenkins obtained in their study. But whereas they only produced 2.8 per cent of "mixed" grouping, the Home Office study produced 51 per cent. It also showed very little correlation between the behaviour syndromes and the upbringing patterns (see Tables 1–8). A socialized delinquency syndrome, as defined by Hewitt and Jenkins, was not found in the Home Office study but confirmation for the other two behavioural syndromes exists.

TABLE 1. BEHAVIOURAL ITEMS

1. Unsocialized aggression syndrome
    (a) Assaultive tendencies
    (b) Initiatory fighting
    (c) Cruelty
    (d) Defiance of authority
    (e) Malicious mischief
    (f) Inadequate guilt feelings

2. Socialized delinquency syndrome
    (a) Bad companions
    (b) Gang activities
    (c) Co-operative stealing[a]
    (d) Furtive stealing[b]
    (e) Habitual school truancy
    (f) Truancy from home
    (g) Staying out late nights
[a] In the H.O. study interpreted as "stealing with others".
[b] In the H.O. study interpreted as "stealing alone".

3. Over-inhibited syndrome
    (a) Seclusiveness
    (b) Shyness
    (c) Apathy
    (d) Worrying
    (e) Sensitiveness
    (f) Submissiveness

TABLE 2. NUMBER OF BOYS CLASSIFIED IN THE BEHAVIOURAL SYNDROMES

	A Unsocialized aggression syndrome	B Socialized delinquency syndrome	C Over-inhibited syndrome	A+B	A+C	B+C	A+B+C	Unclassified	Total
Number	13	64	30	38	11	56	34	28	274
%	4·7	23·4	10·9	13·9	4·1	20·4	12·4	10·2	100

TABLE 3. THE INTER-ITEM CORRELATIONS (PRODUCT MOMENT) OF THE BEHAVIOURAL SYNDROMES

I. The unsocialized aggression syndrome

Frequency		a	b	c	d	e	f
49	(a) Assaultive tendencies		·40c	·44c	·23c	·14a	·14a
113	(b) Initiatory fighting			·25c	·42c	·19b	·20c
35	(c) Cruelty				·26c	·18b	·09
105	(d) Defiance of authority					·18b	·16b
88	(e) Malicious mischief						·17b
149	(f) Inadequate guilt feelings						

II. The socialized delinquency syndrome

Frequency	a	b	c	d	e	f	g
192 (a) Association with undesirable companions		·35ᶜ	−·02	·08	·23ᶜ	−·18ᵇ	·31ᶜ
75 (b) Gang activities			−·08	−·03	·19ᵇ	−·14ᵃ	·16ᵇ
150 (c) Habitual or frequent school truancy				·13ᵃ	·26ᶜ	·02	−·13ᵃ
79 (d) Running away from home					·31ᶜ	·15ᵃ	−·15ᵃ
104 (e) Staying out late at night						·03	−·05
166 (f) Solitary stealing							−·32ᶜ
195 (g) Co-operative stealing							

III. The over-inhibited syndrome

Frequency	a	b	c	d	e	f
92 (a) Seclusiveness		·54ᶜ	·34ᶜ	·35ᶜ	·18ᵇ	·18ᵇ
127 (b) Shyness or timidity			·45ᶜ	·39ᶜ	·21ᶜ	·30ᶜ
114 (c) Apathy				·29ᶜ	·06	·28ᶜ
135 (d) Worrying					·51ᶜ	·26ᶜ
118 (e) Sensitiveness						·27ᶜ
66 (f) Submissiveness						

ᵃ Significant at the 5 per cent level.
ᵇ Significant at the one per cent level.
ᶜ Significant at the 0·1 per cent level.

TABLE 4. UPBRINGING ITEMS

Hewitt and Jenkins Items	Items used in the Home Office Study

1. Pattern of parental rejection

Illegitimate pregnancy	Illegitimate birth
Pregnancy unwanted by father ⎱ Pregnancy unwanted by mother ⎰	Boy's birth unwanted or deplored
Post-delivery rejection by father	Father without affection or showed dislike for boy
Post-delivery rejection by mother	Mother without affection or showed dislike for boy
Mother unwilling to accept parental role	Mother neglected boy and allowed him to run wild
Mother sexually unconventional	Mother sexually loose, promiscuous, lived with extra-marital partners
Mother openly hostile to child	Mother harsh or cruel to boy
Loss of contact with both natural parents	At time of committal the boy did not live with either of his parents

2. Pattern of parental negligence and exposure to delinquent behaviour

Interior of home unkempt	Boy's home dirty and ill-kept
Irregular home routine	No information
Lack of supervision	No information
Father's discipline lax	Father neglected boy and allowed him to run wild
Mother's discipline lax	Mother neglected boy and allowed him to run wild
Mother mentally inadequate	Mother mentally dull or deficient
Father's discipline harsh	Father over-critical and disciplined boy excessively
Mother's discipline harsh	Mother over-critical and disciplined boy excessively
Mother shielding	Mother over-indulged or over-protected boy
Sibling reputedly delinquent	No information
Sibling officially delinquent	Sibling with criminal record
Urban deteriorated area	No information

3. Pattern of family repression

Father's discipline inconsistent	Father was capricious in disciplining the boy—lax one moment, harsh the next
Father hypercritical	Father over-critical and disciplined him excessively
Father unsociable	No information
Mother unsociable	No information
Mother dominating ⎱ Mother compensated rejection ⎰	Mother over-indulged and over-protected the boy
Sibling rivalry	No information

Table 5. Number of Boys Classified in the Upbringing Patterns

	X Pattern of parental rejection	Y Pattern of parental negligence and exposure to delinquent behaviour	Z Pattern of family repression	X+Y	X+Z	Y+Z	X+Y+X	Unclassified	Total
Number	17	22	78	10	4	74	20	49	274
%	6·2	8·0	28·5	3·6	1·5	27·0	7·3	17·9	100

Table 6. The Inter-item Correlations (Product Moment) of the Upbringing Patterns

I. Pattern of parental rejection

Frequency	a	b	c	d	e	f	g	h
37 (a) Illegitimate birth		·45[c]	·14[a]	·00	-·06	·34[c]	-·07	·24[c]
29 (b) Boys birth unwanted			·15[a]	·13[a]	-·03	·10	-·06	·26[c]
62 (c) Father without affection				·28[c]	·08	·04	·15[a]	-·03
39 (d) Mother without affection					·15[a]	·05	·16[b]	-·09
126 (e) Mother neglected boy						·12[a]	-·01	-·07
45 (f) Mother promiscuous							-·03	·13[a]
9 (g) Mother harsh or cruel								-·06
30 (h) Boy did not live with parents at time of admission								

II. *Pattern of parental negligence and exposure to delinquent behaviour*

Frequency	a	b	c	d	e	f	g	h
41 (a) Boy's home dirty		·20^c	·19^b	·15^a	−·11	·01	−·01	−·01
117 (b) Father neglected boy			·56^c	·16^b	−·06	−·06	−·06	−·11
126 (c) Mother neglected boy				·27^c	−·10	−·05	−·03	−·19^b
39 (d) Mother dull or mentally deficient					−·02	−·03	−·09	−·19^b
55 (e) Father over-critical						·19^b	·12	−·01
19 (f) Mother over-critical							−·11	−·03
113 (g) Mother over-indulged and over-protected boy								−·15^b
132 (h) Sibling with criminal record								

III. *Pattern of family repression*

Frequency	a	b	c
73 Father capricious in disciplining boy		·07	·00
55 Father over-critical			·12
113 Mother over-indulged and over-protected boy			

^{a} Significant at the 5 per cent level.
^{b} Significant at the 1 per cent level.
^{c} Significant at the 0·1 per cent level.

Table 7. Correlation between the Behavioural Syndromes and Upbringing Patterns

	Unsocialized aggression syndrome	Socialized delinquency syndrome	Over-inhibited syndrome
Pattern of parental rejection	·06	·00	·01
Pattern of parental negligence and exposure to delinquent behaviour	−·07	−·10	·07
Pattern of family repression	·09	·00	·04

Table 8. Distribution of Boys between the Behaviour Syndromes and Upbringing Patterns

	Unsocialized aggression syndrome	Socialized delinquency syndrome	Over-inhibited syndrome	Others	Total
Pattern of parental rejection	0	4	2	11	17
Pattern of parental negligence and exposure to delinquent behaviour	0	2	4	16	22
Pattern of family repression	6	18	10	44	78
Others	7	40	14	96	157
Total	13	64	30	167	274

Dr. Keith Wardrop (XXVII), Director of the Forensic Psychiatric Clinic, Glasgow, finds it useful to divide delinquent adolescents into four groups, based mainly on aetiological factors but keeping in mind also practical treatment possibilities. The groups, described below, overlap to some extent.

a. *Organic*

There is, first of all, the group whose delinquency has a mainly (though not wholly) organic basis, the result of some degree of brain damage. This is a fairly clear-cut group, with typical histories and behaviour patterns. There is frequently an early history of birth trauma, early injury or illness, such as encephalitis, followed by a history of infant difficulties of all kinds, an improvement during childhood, though a persistent tendency to hyperkinetic behaviour, poor muscular co-ordination, various developmental retardations, with more behaviour difficulties beginning to occur round about the time of puberty. These usually take the form of outbursts of temper and overtly delinquent behaviour, often apparently motiveless.

Such conditions may sometimes be associated with epilepsy, temporal lobe epilepsy, or specific brain damage, but more generally with non-specific findings both on neurological and on EEG examination. In such cases, although no localizing neurological symptoms are found, it appears that the behaviour difficulties result from brain maldevelopment and a degree of physiological immaturity.

There is no clear correlation between this and actual delinquency since many such cases in fact do not become delinquent. Because of their poor impulse control, however, as well as for other reasons, they are potentially delinquent. Whether or not they actually commit offences often depends on the immediate surroundings. Sometimes in such cases there is also a history of disturbance in family relationships. It seems that a member of the family who is particularly at risk because of even a mild degree of organic impairment is more likely to become anti-social in his behaviour.

This group is not confined to any one socio-economic level, and may contain representatives of all classes of the population. Offences tend to be aggressive rather than aquisitive, and may involve deviant sex behaviour. The interactional setting depends on the social class background, but there is generally no persistent interaction with a delinquent sub-culture, nor is there usually a self-image of criminality.

Some cases, however, particularly where there is much family tension, tend increasingly to become indentified with a delinquent group.

Another feature of this group is the shallowness of affect, the complete incapacity for affectional relationships or social identification, the poor capacity for abstract thinking and a general symptomatology resembling that of the adult psychopath. It is not advisable to use the term "psychopathy" as a diagnosis in any teenage delinquent, at least until such time as normal development should have taken place. It is obvious, however, that teenagers in the above group—i.e. one in which there are organic causal factors—may well tend to psychopathic character disorders. In this they overlap with persons in the next group.

b. *The Grossly Deprived Group*

This group contains a very clear-cut type of adolescent delinquent. The history is usually of illegitimacy, or rejection at an early stage for other reasons, followed by a very deprived first few years in life, involving child-care, frequent fostering, placement in children's homes, etc., with an increasing rejection by the adult community as the child gets older. The behavioural pattern is a typical one of hostility in all social relationships, increasing as the child gets older, low impulse control, low tolerance of frustration and a tendency to immediate impulse gratification.

There are sub-types of this group which show a specific symptomatology: for example, the tendency to immediate impulse gratification often takes the form of thieving from an early age and this gradually becomes compulsive stealing. This is a more marked characteristic in boys than in girls, perhaps because acquisitive behaviour is culturally more normal for the male than the female.

Girls who have become compulsive thieves constitute a quite distinct clinical group, and one which is very difficult to treat. Such girls invariably present a picture of a very deprived, affectionless childhood. Stealing begins at an early age, apparently as a compensatory mechanism. It serves the purpose of replacing, to some extent, the emotional satisfaction of which the child is deprived, and is also a means of expressing hostility against the community. This in itself is so satisfying that the act becomes habitual, and is reinforced at the time of puberty. In such girls, compulsive stealing often becomes a sexual sublimation as well. This type of girl delinquent is very different in her attitudes to sexual behaviour (though not always in the actual behaviour itself) from the more common type of female delinquent who is involved in much promiscuous behaviour.

Drug users are another sub-type in this group. Common to both boys and girls in this very deprived group is the obvious use of oral means to achieve emotional gratification. By the middle teens, many have become at least potential (if not actual) addicts to alcohol or to drugs. In both sexes, they invariably show a generalized hostility and distrust of society as a whole. Another commonly noted feature is that their level of self-evaluation is extremely low; they regard themselves as being totally worthless creatures. This is even more noticeable in the case of girls.

This type most commonly belongs to socio-economic class 5, and an approximate description, according to Don Gibbon's four-dimensional assessment, would be:

(i) Offence behaviour—persistently anti-social including all forms of criminal activity.
(ii) Interactional setting. Tend to drift into delinquent areas, but form no lasting attachments anywhere.
(iii) Self-image is of isolation and rejection by society, personal worthlessness, rather than a definite criminal indentification.
(iv) The attitudes to community agencies are hostility and distrust.

c. *Emotionally Disturbed Group*

This term is used to describe an equally clear-cut type of teenage delinquent, whose delinquency originates from and in fact represents part or all of the symptomatology of an underlying severe emotional disturbance or of a severe neurotic reaction. Though teenagers in this group are not so grossly damaged, from the point of view of personality development, as those in the previous group, there is usually a history of some degree of deprivation, rejection, parental separation, disharmony or hostility in relationships in the early years. Typically, the history shows emotional disturbance in early development, frequently connected with oedipal relationships. The result of these disturbances at puberty is a delay in emotional, particularly in psycho-sexual maturation, so there is still some confusion over sexual identification. This leads to behaviour designed to over-emphasize sexual identification—i.e. aggressive or acquisitive delinquency in the male or a tendency to promiscuity in the female without any real emotional satisfaction in the relationships.

Offences tend to follow the above patterns in the male and female respectively. The interactional setting varies, but commonly such teenagers come from average home backgrounds with reasonable standards and relationships. They are often members of youth clubs and other organizations, and in general are not identified with delinquent sub-cultures. All social classes are represented in this type, though social classes 3 and 4 are perhaps the commonest. The self-image is not one of delinquency, but can be one of isolation, difference from fellows, etc., while attitudes to community agencies are inconsistent.

d. *Family Problem Group*

This group contains adolescents whose personality and development follow the average pattern, in whom there is no degree of individual emotional disturbance, but whose delinquency is a reaction to interpersonal tension in family relationships. From the point of view of symptomatology, this type is far from homogeneous, several different patterns of underlying family pathology being exhibited.

(a) In boys a frequent pattern is the unconscious encouragement of delinquency (and the emotional satisfaction derived therefrom) on the part of the mother. Consciously, the mother expresses shock at the son's behaviour, and tends to be a nagger in the family circle. Such mothers tend to deny the fact of delinquency in the family except when a crisis arises, when they over-react.

(b) An over-strict father who is also unconsciously identifying with the son's delinquency and getting satisfaction therefrom. This, however, is too threatening to his carefully built-up defences; hence his severe reaction to the boy. This reaction fulfils two functions: (i) it supports his own super-ego, and (ii) it is likely to encourage the son's further rebellion.

(c) In girls the most commonly found pattern is that of a bad relationship between the adolescent girl and her father which has arisen at puberty. In this, the father's emotional involvement, though unconscious, is quite apparent. The other side of this picture is the mother's more overt hostility to the girl without any conscious but very obvious unconscious reasons.

(d) Also in girls, a less frequent but quite definite pattern is that of extreme hostility and rejection between the girl and her mother from an early age, with an unconscious rejection of feminine identification, leading at puberty towards promiscuity, but also to the adoption of delinquency as being a male pattern culturally.

Young people of this type are most commonly met with in social classes 2 and 3. The offences usually take the form of theft, often of a motiveless kind. Their interactional setting varies; it is usually among their own social cultural background, with appropriate identification. But where family tension is very high, there may be transient phases of interaction with delinquent sub-cultures. The self-image is not normally that of criminality, but one of strong adherence to the adolescent peer-group.

e. *Situational Delinquency Group*

This term is used to cover the heterogeneous group of teenage delinquents in whom there is no psychiatric or emotional problem, but who are typical products of their cultural background. Depending on this latter, the offences will be predominantly acquisitive or aggressive. Gibbons draws an interesting distinction, particularly in relation to the interactional setting, between "predatory gang" and "conflict gang". In Scotland there tends to be an overlap between these two types, but there does remain a basic distinction in that the essentially aggressive gang is the product of a less organized cultural background, with shifting mores, and violent behaviour as the norm. Acquisitive gangs, on the other hand, tend to belong to a rather more organized and settled culture, where violent behaviour is less tolerated, but acquisitive behaviour is an accepted norm. In both, the attitude to the rest of the community and to community agencies is one of hostility and a mild, though endemic degree of cultural paranoia is found.

3. ASPECTS OF ADDICTION

Dr. Wardrop's attempts to relate personality type to social environment in the genesis and treatment of delinquency is echoed by another psychiatrist, Dr. Griffith Edwards (X), in his study of the interaction of personality and environment in alcohol addiction.

Personality and the Origin of Addiction

Understanding the personality of the addict is, of course, essential to a comprehension of how he becomes addicted. Personality also bears on what befalls any human being after he has become addicted and influences the chance and quality of his recovery.

To criticize in detail the various attempts to define the addictive personality is not a worthwhile exercise. Generalization has certainly been here one of the great pit-falls, with different authors describing addicts of very special types in special settings—the imprisoned narcotic addict, for instance—and drawing wide conclusions. Rorschach or other projective tests have been used and control groups from appropriate social backgrounds have seldom been studied. All that can be salvaged from this literature is contained in two postulates:

(a) The non-specific element of anxiety can be causal. The anxious person—anxious for any reason—may use drugs or drink to relieve his tension, with the psychodynamics of the anxiety real and complex but the dynamics of the drug-taking not so very much more obscure than the motivation of any of us who takes aspirin for a headache.

(b) Drug-taking can have many specific dynamic reasons, and for each individual patient these must be understood. For one adolescent, drugs may be aggression against the self, while in another case addiction may be aggression against parents, and any attempt to fit all cases into one neat pattern will be totally misleading.

Our own data illustrates the problem: the Maudsley Personality Inventory N (neuroticism) scores on alcoholics attending the Maudsley Hospital were significantly higher than those found in a normal population; and a similar result was found when the neuroticism (N) score of Alcoholics Anonymous members in London was ascertained. When, however, the neuroticism score of a private patient group—consisting largely of wealthy executives—was measured, it was found to be in no way raised. These studies point to the danger of generalization but also incidentally lead on to a consideration of the interaction of environment and personality in the genesis of addictions.

Why should the executives have had a normal N score? One may

D

guess that the answer is that they had become addicted largely because their business and social life had exposed them to heavy drinking, this being a reflection of anxiety about specific problems. To talk about disease being the result of interaction between personality and environment is not more than a truism. What is badly needed is mensuration of the proposed equation which underlies this truism. It would, for instance, be of interest to know whether alcoholics in a country with measured heavy drinking pressures or in which alcohol was (measurably) cheap show less (measured) personality deviance than alcoholics in a country where drinking pressures are moderate. Similarly, it should be established whether doctor narcotic addicts who have ready access to drugs show less personality abnormality than narcotic addicts for whom similar environmental pressures are not operative. In the personality–environment postulate we seem sometimes to be in danger of being stuck at the point of platitude. Here the study of addiction is not only important in its own right but can offer a way in to precise measurement of the *relative* importance of the two groups of factors.

Personality and what happens to the Addict

Addiction does not exist *in vacuo:* one is always dealing with a person who is addicted. The behaviour of the addict, the social disruption he suffers, and even the physical complications are as much determined by the personality as by the addiction. Again, however, we have to bring in a personality–environment equation, for the fate of the addict will be influenced by such facts as his social class and social stability.

In a study of 306 members of Alcoholics Anonymous, neuroticism (N) and extraversion (E) scores were measured on the M.P.I., social stability on the Strauss–Bacon scale, and recorded social class in terms of the Registrar-General's classification. A correlation analysis has then been made between these variables and twenty-two "complications" of excessive drinking. It was found that the N score was very highly related $P< 0.001$) to a subject's having been in prison because of drinking or having attempted suicide because of drinking. The N score was highly related ($P< 0.01$) to sleeping rough, drinking crude spirit and developing a peptic ulcer; and significantly ($P< 0.05$) related to pawning, stealing and having been arrested more than five times for drunkenness.

The importance of personality in determining what happens to the alcohol addict must, however, not be allowed to overshadow the importance of environmental factors. For all the instances of complications mentioned above (except for drinking crude spirit and peptic ulcer), it was found that subjects of higher class were less likely to have suffered the complications. A very similar statement could be made about the influence of higher social stability. The data on peptic ulcer perhaps provide the most interesting example of what can be gained from an analysis of this sort: the question as to whether a peptic ulcer in alcoholics is due to personality or to the corrosive action of alcohol has been extensively debated in the literature, and the present finding that the N score relates to ulceration while the length of drinking history does not show a significant correlation seems strong evidence that underlying personality is indeed the more important causal factor.

Thinking along these lines, one might hazard the guess that because only some teenagers who take purple hearts go on to more serious drug abuse or fall foul of the law, this could be shown by a similar correlation analysis, explicable in terms of personality and environmental measures. The M.P.I. is, of course, a relatively crude instrument, but that a significant correlation can be obtained on the N scale hints at the rich possibilities of a more sophisticated approach.

Personality and Recovery

Some addicts make a seemingly permanent recovery and some do not. The truism is to say that those who do not are of "poorer personality". Experience also suggests that recovery very much depends on the social setting to which the addict returns. Again, however, how is one to go beyond the recurrent variation on the personality–environment postulate and achieve mensuration?

A recent study followed up forty hospital-treated alcohol addicts over one year and rated the year's outcome score (OS) for each subject in terms of accumulated monthly scores: each month a patient could score a maximum of 2 points so that 24 points represented the year's maximum. N and E are each scored on a 48-point and social stability (SS) on a 4-point scale. A regression equation was then calculated to relate these variables.

Although N was significantly negatively and E significantly positively correlated with outcome, the contribution of these two factors was so small in relation to the dominance of social stability (SS) that, with very little loss of accuracy, outcome could be predicted on SS alone.

This study thus shows that in alcoholic addiction the environment may be more important than personality in determining outcome— at least with this particular range of personality factors.

Extreme caution is, of course, necessary; for the measures employed are all crude and incomplete, and it is probably best to regard this study as a preliminary essay in method rather than as anything definitive. To suggest, on the basis of these findings, that treatment aimed at influencing the environment might be more effective than treatment aimed at influencing the personality, is to put forward no more than a very tentative hypothesis.

Synthesis

The use of rating scales and statistical methods should not be taken as implying a disregard for the value of the insights that come from the study of the dynamics of the individual cases. Clinical experience suggests that there is much waiting to be worked out on the possibilities of spontaneous ego maturation when the patient breaks his drug habit, and on the profound and often regressive personality disturbances which result from continued drug-taking. That maturation and disturbances are not simply related to cessation of intoxication or prolonged chemical insult is suggested by very similar findings in the pathological gambler.

In essence, what all statistical findings and dynamic insights today point to is that in studying addiction we should not make our focus the drug but the person and the person's setting. This is not an overstatement and one need not go so far as to assert that "alcohol has nothing to do with alcoholism", a claim which is to be regarded as no more than an epigram. Drugs have a lot to do with drug addiction, but it is a corrective to a too exclusive concern with chemistry to talk to the narcotic addict and find that he has many times sweated his way through the withdrawal symptoms only to go back again on to the drugs for some motive which he senses as half hidden or because, as he tells us, he lives down a particular street.

The notion of addiction is extended to certain mentally abnormal recidivists by Dr. Donald West (XXVIII). He holds that some recidivists are specifically "addicted" to a particular criminal habit, without necessarily showing any widespread psychopathic disturbance in their family life or in their behaviour at work. It sometimes happens that a person who has demonstrated his ability to function adequately in many of the social roles required of the mature adult, nevertheless exhibits a compulsive urge to some particular anti-social behaviour, such as shoplifting, sexual deviation or taking illicit drugs.

These habits often serve to relieve tension, and afford a primitive form of escape from difficult life situations which the individual fears that he cannot cope with. Once established, the self-comforting pleasures such habits bring may become an end in themselves, and the habits may persist long after the situation which brought them about has solved itself. A few of these compulsive recidivists are persons who could well manage without their compulsions; and these make good candidates for psychiatric treatment, perhaps by de-conditioning techniques. Many others, unfortunately, persist in their compulsions because they are desperately frustrated or unhappy about some aspect of their lives. Their disorder may not be so obvious or widespread as that of the classical psychopath; but, nevertheless, it is often severe and calls for extensive help.

4. SOCIAL THEORIES

The paper read by Mr. Stanley Cohen (VII), a sociologist, on behalf of Dr. David Downes, is concerned with recent sociological theories of delinquency; and particularly with Cloward and Ohlin's opportunity structure theory. This has clearly made much less impact on thinking in this country than in the United States.

Opportunity structure theory (though presumably considered monolithic by Dr. Walker) for the first time integrates previous sociological theories with a coherent whole, and yet it remains flexible. In its original form it was used to explain *gang* delinquency. But now it seems likely that it was equally appropriate to the explanation of other forms of delinquency.

The three main components of opportunity structure theory are:

(1) The ecological theories of the twenties and thirties.
(2) The anomie theory as developed by Merton.
(3) Cohen's two-pronged theory of status frustration and the delinquent sub-culture.

Empirical research has shown that none of these three theories by themselves are wholly satisfactory in explaining the phenomenon of delinquency. Opportunity theory combines all three, although it discards the status frustration component of Cohen's theory. The main argument of opportunity structure theory can be summarized as follows:

> The primary impetus towards delinquency springs from the anomie strain in American society, generated by a culture which chiefly stresses the goal of money-success and yet denies to a substantial proportion of the population the opportunity to achieve it.

Whereas Cohen considered the school to be the most important component in the problem of adjustment, Cloward and Ohlin saw the problems centred largely round the job market and housing. They maintained that the continuance of criminal activity depended upon the presence of organized adult crime as well as upon the degree of integration between criminal and non-criminal elements in the population. Thus fighting gangs are most likely to change since they receive little structural support in the community, whereas retreatist behaviour, such as drug addiction, is more resistant to change since it is integrated on a commercial basis with adult criminality. It is important to recognize that Cloward and Ohlin were trying to account for different *rates* and different *types* of delinquency; and not to answer the question "What makes one boy delinquent whilst his neighbour goes straight?" Nevertheless, their theory does allow scope for the explanation of variations in delinquent behaviour.

Some critics have pointed out that the theory of opportunity structure is so novel and apparently so complete that people have tended not to notice that it lacks a factual basis. Dr. Downes claims that such criticisms ignore the extent to which the factual basis for the theory is implicit in the separate parts which together make it a whole. The first basic assumption in the theory is the association between low social status and delinquency. Virtually all available statistics confirm this view, despite some evidence of the growth of middle-class delinquency. The second basic assumption is that delinquency is both generated and maintained by the sub-cultural process. The existing evidence supports this view also.

Whereas previous theories have viewed the delinquent event as one which plunges the non-delinquent into delinquency for all time, opportunity structure theory allows for what Matza refers to as "drift" —the evident fact that permanent delinquency may not be the result of single delinquent acts. The limited amount of research carried out to date suggests that much of the theory holds good, though it may be necessary to discard the elements of status frustration and alienation as important causal factors. Possibly status frustration is more appropriate as an explanation of middle-class delinquency.

How relevant is the theory to British experience? There are obvious cultural differences between American and British society. Two factors predominate: the first is that, in Britain, social class is still a much stronger social factor than in America. The second is that American society is divided by ethnicity as much as by social class, a state of affairs not paralleled here. Finally, adult crime in Britain is far less organized and less successful than in the United States, and so the opportunity structure is less attractive and also less accessible.

On such grounds, it is suggested that delinquency in Britain will be an outgrowth of working-class culture rather than a result of socially induced strain, and that it will be milder and less virulent than in the United States. The question is therefore posed why it is necessary (at least in Britain) to modify the working-class culture explanations of Mays and Morris in this country and Walter Miller in America. The working-class culture theory maintains that socialization in female-based households is an important component in delinquency, and Miller further identifies a number of "focal concerns" which characterize lower-class culture. This theory maintains that delinquency flows from absolute position in the social hierarchy rather than from relative deprivation *vis-á-vis* others. To Miller and Mays, delinquency will continue as long as the cleavage between life situations of manual and non-manual workers persists.

The objections to such a theory are that whilst it may account for the origins of delinquent sub-cultures, it no longer accounts for their continuance, nor for changes in form. If Miller is right, one would expect much higher rates of delinquency in Britain where the working class constitutes a larger sociological majority in the population. Furthermore, delinquency should be declining as the proportion of working-class persons in the population declines. But changes in geographical mobility, the loosening of community ties, changes in the educational system, full juvenile employment and greater spending power by young people, have all created a situation very different from that which obtained when working-class sub-cultural theories first appeared. Such theories are consequently less relevant nowadays.

Finally, there is the question of teenage culture, defined as "working-class culture subtly transmuted to meet age-specific needs and tastes". There is clearly a greater working-class involvement in teenage culture, in terms of a dissociation from aspirations in all fields—work, school, community activity. It is in the field of leisure that Merton's "goal-means" scheme has to be viewed. Where there is a blockage of opportunity in both work and leisure, it may be necessary to manufacture excitement via risk-taking through delinquency. It may be said that sub-cultural theory has made an important contribution towards a more realistic understanding of the processes involved in conformity and deviance.

5. WHITE-COLLAR CRIME

The problem of conformity and deviance was echoed in Dr. Louis Blom-Cooper's (IV) paper on white-collar crime. This type of crime is seen here through the eyes of a lawyer who is sociologically orientated; and this becomes evident by the analysis of the late Professor E. H. Sutherland's definition of white-collar crime as "crime committed by a person of respectability and high social status in the course of his occupation".

Sutherland's preoccupation with the social status of the offenders —the upper socio-economic classes—obscures the fundamental characteristic of white-collar crime, namely that it is criminal behaviour committed in the course of otherwise lawful occupation. The criminal behaviour is so encapsulated by the circumstances in which it is manifested that it needs either the expert eye to pick it out or the pertinacious sleuth to winkle out the fraudulent element in otherwise conformist conduct. Ordinary crime is naked crime; it never wears the pretence of respectability.

White-collar crime has the veneer of respectability born of community tolerance. Non-conforming social behaviour falls into the spectrum of crime, from the career-type non-conformity to conventional non-conformity through to ideological non-conformity. The first represents normal crime as reflected in the statistical evidence;

the third may represent political crime. It is the second type—what might be termed conventional delinquent behaviour—that is the distinctive feature of white-collar crime.

Each kind of non-conformity consists of deviations which have three related norms. Law is the central norm; the second norm is the element of ethical or idealistic values which are additional to and superimposed on law observance; the third norm is the public tolerance of certain criminal behaviour—tolerated because it occurs in the context of socio-economic life where such conduct is permissible to meet the inconveniences or exigencies of the social order. All white-collar crime is, in varying degrees, implicitly tolerated. Shopkeepers write off losses from embezzlement and shoplifting; theft covered by insurance goes unrecorded or undetected by the police; tax-evasion, to the extent that it is discoverable by the Revenue, is dealt with administratively.

Is conventional crime, then, crime? There are four basic reasons for not officially recognizing the criminality in conventional crime:

(1) The impersonality of the crime. White-collar crime is directed not at any person but at the community at large.
(2) The offenders are not readily identifiable with the stereotype of a criminal. There is a mixture of readily perceivable admiration and envy as well as distaste for the offence.
(3) The penal sanctions are singularly inappropriate for the white-collar criminal.
(4) The morality of white-collar crime as it is seen by lawyers and by the public may induce public tolerance, although there may also be increased public intolerance.

The criminal statistics fail to reveal the vast area of white-collar crime. So long as our view of crime remains so one-dimensional, our penal system will remain unjust. We will continue to visit heavy penal sanctions on the persistent petty thief while the persistent petty embezzler will tend to avoid the clutches of the criminal law. This is the more reprehensible since it is the white-collar criminal who causes the greatest disequilibrium of our economic stability. As Thurmann Arnold, in his *Folklore of Capitalism*, brought home to a generation of Americans, it was the financier not the gangster, "Insult not Capone", who wrecked the financial structure of Chicago in the thirties.

Mr. Morris Finer, Q.C. (XII), takes Dr. Blom-Cooper's theoretical remarks into the field of the current practice of white-collar crime. In particular, he concerns himself with the company fraud which is here defined to mean a dishonest transaction inflicting loss on others, in the scheme of which the interposition of one or more limited liability companies plays an essential part.

This definition may cover conduct which the law does not make subject to a criminal penalty or to even a civil remedy. This is consistent with some of the views advanced in criminological writing on white-collar crime, but is justified also from the point of view of the company lawyer as indicating his practical difficulties in working in a legal continuum of blurred boundaries and values.

There is an historical contrast between the broadly successful efforts to accommodate limited liability with the social and economic demands of the welfare state and the failure to eradicate the abuse of limited liability as an instrument of fraud. This failure is a reflection of a paradoxical adherence to an attitude of *laissez-faire* in the regulatory parts of company law.

Various characteristics of the law illustrate this attitude well.

There is, first of all, the persistence of gaps and ambiguities on an unacceptable scale, as may be shown by reference to sections 190, 332 and 54 of the Companies Act, 1948.

Section 190 provides that, with exceptions, it shall not be lawful for a company to make a loan to any person who is its director or a director of its holding company. Yet although a loan in contravention of the section is expressed to be "not lawful", nowhere in the Act is there any sanction which attaches to the making or the receipt of such a loan. Accordingly (unless the facts can support a Common Law conspiracy count against two or more persons who have agreed to make the unlawful loan) breach of the section can give rise to civil liabilities only. Next, the section has no application at all where the loan, instead of being made to a director, is made to another company controlled by the director of the lending company. Finally, a company may be controlled *de facto* by a person who has never been formally appointed a director, but in accordance with whose instructions the *de jure* directors never fail to act. But a loan to such a person is not caught by the section.

The policy of the section is clear. It is aimed at a transaction which may often be innocent, but which so lends itself to improper purposes that it is thought better to make it subject to a general prohibition.

But the heart of the legislator has failed him in the event, and the consequence is a lattice-work rule that is wide open to evasion.

Section 332 deals with fraudulent trading. Subsection (1) provides that if, in the course of a winding up of a company, it appears that any business of the company has been carried on with intent to defraud creditors, the court may declare that any persons who were knowingly party to the carrying on of the business in that manner shall be personally responsible without any limitation of liability for all or any of the debts or other liabilities of the company. Subsection (3) provides, further, that every such person shall be liable on conviction to imprisonment or fine.

Thus, on the face of it, section 332 provides a powerful instrument for restitution and punishment in the key area where the legally limited personal liability of members may encourage them to abuse the legally unlimited amount of credit which the company is free to obtain. The same conduct gives rise to both civil and criminal consequences; and the essential element in both cases is the presence of an intent to defraud creditors.

What constitutes this intent? Judicial guidance comes from Maugham, J. who has informed us that this intent connotes "actual dishonesty, involving according to current notions of fair trading among commercial men, real moral blame".

But the lawyer remains in a dilemma. His clients are the directors of a trading company with a respectable history. The company has small reserves and has suffered a bad season. Next season, if trade revives and there is no increase in purchase tax (as it is rumoured there may be), all should be well. Meantime, the company needs to purchase materials for next season's products. Thus, there is a real and appreciated risk, not possible to calculate precisely, that the suppliers of such materials will not, in the event, be paid. Does the exposure of creditors to a contingency of this kind involve real moral blame according to current notions of fair trading? Will the conclusion be the same if the chairman of the board happens, some years previously, to have taken a charge over the assets of the company to secure advances by him, so that if the company does become insolvent the value of the materials purchased will be used to pay him off instead of the creditors at large?

On the criminal side, all these doubts are resolved in a simple fashion. The average number of prosecutions brought under section 332 each year is only about a dozen. This low figure is not an indication of the standards of commercial purity, but of the obscurity of the law.

The third example from the 1948 Act is section 54. This provides that it shall not be lawful for a company to give, whether directly or indirectly, any financial assistance for the purposes of or in connection with a purchase made or to be made by any person of or for any shares in the company. Some of the implications of the section may be considered by reference to a fictitious illustration in which, for ease of understanding, the facts and figures have been much over-simplified.

A rubber company, unhappy over the political future in Malaysia, has sold all its estates and brought all the proceeds home. It has £1,000,000 in the bank and is existing, rather like a capon on the eve of execution, in a state of prosperous immobility. The directors own 30 per cent of the shares and the rest are widely distributed among a public consisting largely of the relicts of clergymen and colonial civil servants. A take-over bidder ascertains from the directors (whose decision is eased by the promise of substantial compensation payments for loss of office) that they are ready to accept 20s. each for their own shares and to recommend a similar offer to outside share-holders. Outside shareholders who own, say, another 25 per cent of the shares, do accept this offer. The bidder can now acquire 55 per cent of the issued capital at a total cost, at 20s. per share, of say £600,000. For this outlay, he can get control over £1,000,000. His only problem now is to find £600,000; which problem has, from the start, presented itself to him, as a practical man, as how he can get £600,000 out of the company's money in the bank without infringing section 54.

In order to do this, the co-operation of a bank will usually be necessary, and was, at least until the State Building Society case in 1960, obtainable by the operator with comparatively little difficulty. The pinnacle of the operation is reached on a single day, at a series of meetings succeeding each other over many hours, at which resolutions are passed, minutes signed, drafts exchanged, contracts executed, directors resign, new ones appear, all in accordance with pages of an agenda in which the order of every step is, with an eye on the section, set down like the choreography of a ballet.

Gyrations of this sort naturally involve the risk that the performers will trip over themselves and incur a hurt; and section 54, unlike section 190, indeed provides a penalty for its breach. Such a breach can, and has in fact in several cases during the past few years, involved amounts in six and seven figures. The maximum penalty is a fine of £100.

Another relevant characteristic of the company law concerns directors. The duties of directors are fixed by reference to minimal standards of personal competence and behaviour. The professional bodies show little inclination in favour of raising the standard. Section 188 of the 1948 Act, which enables delinquent directors to be barred from office, is rarely applied. Then there is the fact that the law and the courts proceed upon the notion of a company as a microcosm of political democracy. The practical effect is to expose shareholders to unfair treatment, as may be illustrated by reference to section 210 of the 1948 Act.

There is also comparatively little public supervision over the conduct of company affairs. The apparatus of supervision is essentially private. The consequences are illustrated by reference to the position of auditors and of the liquidator in a winding-up.

Even where a case for investigation or evidence of an offence for prosecution has emerged, the existing enforcement agencies, mainly by reason of understaffing, are inadequate for their task. The control of company fraud does not so much require additions to an existing patchwork of laws, as a fundamental re-thinking of the philosophy upon which the laws should be based. Limited liability is not a natural right, but a privilege deriving from the community; and the regulative system should proceed from this basic premise.

6. GAMES THEORY

The last summary of the papers in this section on theories is really outside Dr. Walker's survey. It is Mr. Sargeaunt's (XXIII) paper on techniques in the control of crime. As Chief Scientific Advisor to the Home Office he has in recent years interested himself particularly in police work; and this leads him to pose quite different questions about delinquency from those of the psychologists or sociologists.

One of the basic principles of science is to ask "How" before asking "Why"—the Galilean revolution. Have "orthodox" criminologists yet answered the "hows" of crime? Do they know the ways by which people actually undertake crime and the decisions and skills by which they finally come to bring off a burglary or a larceny? The search for the indirect causes and the indirect correlations of past circumstances that could produce these present decisions and these present skills is, at this stage, premature. Most criminologists have sought for these indirect social and psychological causes of crime despite Lombroso, the founder of criminology, having originally asked how crime should be immediately pictured.

Though there is no single criminal type there are many partial correlations; correlations not only of character but also of social environment. But nobody created corresponding models of how crimes were actually engineered, since it was the causes of crime and predictions about crime that were being discussed. The usefulness of this phase of criminology has been the large number of detailed statistical studies it has produced. But as a form of analysis and as giving insight, it has proved disappointing. The correlations are so low and the social changes from one decade to another so great that few positive recommendations have or can be made. This is unsatisfactory.

We ought, indeed, to go back to Lombroso's original question and ask what are the mechanisms of crime. In studying what information the police need to solve a crime, we have necessarily had to ask ourselves how the criminal tries to prevent this information falling into the hands of the police; how he plans his crime; what skills he needs; and what decisions he must take. In other words, it is necessary to start with the crime and work backwards from that point. Just as a poet is best first studied by his poetry, an artist by his art, so may a criminal by his crimes.

This sort of approach is already used in the study of murder. But it can be applied to other types of criminal behaviour. It is possible to set up a "Decision Tree" model; and this allows all kinds of partial correlations to be fed in at the initial point of what is really a mechanical "how" model.

The police can only hope to solve a crime against property by obtaining certain information. The criminal's skill, therefore, consists in the ability to deny access to, or otherwise to nullify, the information; and also on his own knowledge of police information. In the face of this, the police strategy is to improve the availability and nature of information; and this, in turn, tends to lead to improved skills by the criminal. His skill has components due to environment, aptitude and the ability to learn from peers—concepts which might prove fruitful points at which police research and criminological research might interact.

A crime can therefore be viewed in terms of the decisions taken by the criminal. They can be analysed in terms of games theory. Games theory can be described as the relationship between risk and pay-off, in economic or in other terms. There is a pay-off matrix when the probability of detection will offset the expectation.

A games-theory model might be criticized on the grounds that the probabilities demanded by this theory are, in effect, subjective judgements and therefore cannot be treated as mathematical probabilities. But this kind of criticism had been made in relation to other processes —for example accounting processes—and had not proved relevant. Another objection is that these kinds of model require a degree of quantification which is hard to imagine. Nevertheless, police research teams have already been able to quantify at the level of "information needed by the police", by introducing a measure analogous to entrophy. This might prove to be the key which could be used to unlock the whole system.

SECOND KEYNOTE LECTURE

III

RESEARCH AND RESEARCH METHODS

T. S. Lodge (XVII)

A characteristic of criminology is that it stretches over a large part of the field of social and psychological sciences, as well as being concerned with the criminal law and judicial proceedings. Research in criminology accordingly breaks down in practice into a large number of quite different kinds of enterprise, and it is at least a reasonable question to ask how far we are entitled to discuss them all in one breath.

As far as research methods are concerned, it is indeed evident that methods must be tailored to the problem and the general situation; one might go so far as to say that in the past some harm has been done by concentration on particular research methods when what was needed was a better appraisal of the problems themselves before deciding how to tackle them. But as regards criminological research in general, there must surely be some way of discussing it as a whole, however heterogeneous it may be. Criminological research workers constitute, after all, a class of persons, just as do, say, administrative civil servants, magistrates or teachers. It should be possible to consider, in general terms, what their function should be and how they and their work should fit into the whole picture of criminological and penal activity.

In the first place, there is a sense in which criminological research should be the eyes and ears of society where crime and the judicial and penal systems are concerned. Research should aim at finding out what is actually happening, as distinct from what is intended to be happening or what is said to be happening.

No one with practical knowledge of these—or probably any other—fields will fail to remember some occasion when he has felt shocked and even incredulous at the naïvete or downright inaccuracy of some statement that he has read or heard about his own work. It must be one of the duties of research to find out and put together facts in a way that is impossible without systematic study. But, the facts having been found out, it must also be the duty of research to communicate them to all who are concerned. This, which is easy enough to say, is one of the most difficult things to do. Partly it is because research workers naturally find it easier to express themselves in the technical terms of their own speciality; partly because the best research workers are by no means always the most articulate; but also because it is a genuinely harassing and extremely time-consuming task to condense and simplify research findings, without unduly distorting them into a form that can be understood by people without technical training. This problem has recently been receiving a lot of discussion. One solution is probably more personal contact between research workers, practitioners and administrators, and another the better training of research workers in this direction. But it may be also that the collation and communication of research results, and the promulgation of summaries of the present state of knowledge in this field or that, can be stimulated by the offer of grants for this purpose to academic criminologists who have a gift for exposition and would find this a suitable and agreeable occupation at some stage of their career.

Secondly, research should investigate how far there are stated objectives of criminal, judicial and penal policy and practice. Where such objectives are not explicitly stated—which is very often the case—there should be research studies to find out what they are, and whether they are right or sufficient.

It is not within the province of research to decide what should be the aims of policy. But it is within its province to explain what aims are in fact being pursued, to show to what extent there is consistency of aim throughout a particular system or between one system and another, and to advise, in the light of study of the subject, on any action that the facts might suggest.

Thirdly, research should examine to what extent the aims of policy are being fulfilled, and arrange for studies to be undertaken to seek better ways of fulfilling them. This third research objective. thus tersely expressed, covers an immense amount of ground, and under this head comes a large proportion of the work that is being done today. I would add just one word; in the search for precision in the measurement of the effectiveness of present practice, let us not forget the search for better ways of fulfilling the aims of policy. There is much room for improvement all round; and research workers, of all people, must carefully avoid being responsible for the freezing of an existing situation. Rather they should foster and suggest constant experimentation.

Lastly, research must find time to study on a fundamental level the determinants of deviant behaviour, and to carry out experiments to test hypotheses about them derived from theory or from previous observation. In this category we can also put the study of mathematical or statistical techniques which may help to solve problems in any criminological field. We do not know whether the more abstract or the more applied kind of research will give the better results, but it would certainly be foolish to neglect either.

If it is accepted that a sizeable part of research activity is going to be used in helping what may be called practitioners with the evaluation of whatever measures they may be taking—say for the prevention of delinquency or in the treatment of offenders—we must recognize a dilemma in which research finds itself. This is that research may have to choose between being completely scientifically sound and being practically useful. In some cases it may be virtually impossible to arrange for the rigorous evaluation of an experiment. In others this may be possible, but if it takes too long to get out the final research results they may be out of date and too late to be of much practical use.

This severely practical problem, affecting criminological research as a whole, and probably most other social research as well, is one to which there can be no simple answer. It would certainly not do for research workers to throw aside scientific respectability and rigour. On the other hand, they should recognize that it may be better to provide provisional or less than perfect information at the time it is wanted than something much better five years too late. Part of the solution may lie in a fuller recognition of research workers as objective observers and interpreters who have the duty to collect information and attempt to interpret it dispassionately, and who will provide a feed-back of facts and their interpretation which should represent the best possible information available at any time as a basis for decisions that must be taken.

There are dangers in this use of research. Unvalidated interpretations of data are always at the risk of being wrong; they may be shown to be wrong when the final research results appear; and every possible effort should always be made to produce scientifically sound results in the end if only so that the correctness of interim interpretations can be checked. But so long as research workers remember and use their scientific training and keep in mind their paramount duty to remain objective and uncommitted, then they should be in a better position than anyone else could be to assess the situation at any time.

So far we have been discussing criminological research as a whole and some questions concerning the general relationship of research to administration and practice. In fact, a research problem will usually present itself in relation to some particular one out of all the many aspects of criminology. These aspects, while all in some way linked together, cover between them a very wide field, and it is difficult to group them in a way that makes it possible to deal with them at anything less than book length.

There may be some advantage in thinking of research questions as coming within one or other of the three following groups:

(1) The nature of crime and juvenile delinquency and their causation and prevention.
(2) Forensic science and the police and judicial systems.
(3) Sentencing and the treatment of offenders.

1. *The nature of crime and juvenile delinquency and their causation and prevention*

The first source of information about crime is the criminal statistics. A Departmental Committee is considering these, and it is possible that we may be able to put into them more information than now about the nature and circumstances of crimes. But we shall still need more information about crime than these statistics will provide. Already some studies have been done on the nature of a criminal society and, with the increase in professional and organized crime, it would seem necessary for much more research to be done on serious property offences and offenders, and the kind of society that generates them.

Sociological and psychological theory has produced a number of hypotheses about the origins of crime and deviant behaviour generally. In this country little has so far been done to test them, and it appears that the Americans, who are responsible for most of the sociological theories, find testing these difficult. Work is at present being done on a psychological hypothesis about deviant behaviour, and I believe it to be important that more of this fundamental kind of research should be done; apart from any help it might give in preventing crime, this is one of the directions from which might come new ideas about the positive reformative treatment of offenders.

One of the things we know little about is the large amount of crime, much of it not very serious, that does not lead to prosecution or caution. Research that has been and is being done on the attitudes of and admissions by young people suggests that many more commit offences than are ever caught. The whole question of the attitude of the public and the police to the less serious offences of dishonesty is one of great interest and importance; some work on public attitudes is being done by the Government Social Survey organization and I hope it will be followed by more. In the meantime, the criminal statistics understate the prevalence of some types of offence, such as the smaller offences of theft, white collar crime, and, of course, motoring offences. There is room for research on the effect of public attitudes towards minor dishonesty on the growth of more serious crime and the establishment of criminal communities. Such research is difficult, and methods for doing it have yet to be developed; but I believe it to be important that it should be done.

The traditional way of seeking the causes of juvenile delinquency has been by comparing a group of delinquents with a matched group of non-delinquents. This control group method may now be in the process of partial supersession by the cohort study, i.e. the long-term following up of a sample of children, preferably from birth, to see how all the circumstances surrounding their birth, family upbringing and education may be related to their development in general and in particular to the development of any tendency towards deviant or criminal behaviour. Studies of this kind clearly have the potential to be extraordinarily fruitful. Many of the technical and logical difficulties associated with control group studies are automatically removed. But it cannot be overlooked that new difficulties of technique and of data collection and analysis are swift to replace the old ones, and that many of these difficulties have not yet been solved. One obvious problem is that any sample, or cohort, which is to contain a reasonable number of delinquents (or should I say recognized delinquents) must itself be of a considerable size. This makes the research expensive; that may mean that a single study must try to cover as much of the ground of child development, education, health and social behaviour as it can; and in doing so it must present itself with perplexities concerning research resources and the handling and interrelation of large quantities of information collected over many years.

But in spite of the difficulties, cohort studies hold out much promise, and much has already been learnt from the National Survey of Child Health and Development which started in 1946 and the National Child Development Study which is concerned with children born in 1958.

It has often been argued that studies of the causation of juvenile delinquency are not likely to lead to practical results for a long time to come and that experimental preventive projects should be undertaken, accompanied by research evaluation, to try out ways of reducing delinquency based on hypotheses as yet unproved. This point of view has been endorsed by various conferences in this and other countries and must in principle command our wholehearted sympathy; the more so since various authorities are all the time taking action which may be preventive, and it is seldom known whether a particular form of action was successful for this purpose or not. It has been possible to begin some projects of this kind, including one in schools, which are places where the United Nations Conference at Frascati in 1962 particularly recommended action. But here again, as with all social research, all is not plain sailing. To test unproved hypotheses involves first selecting the ones to test from all those that exist—an exercise that requires not only judgement but also tact. Again, there are generally considered to be two kinds of juvenile delinquency prevention project between which a choice must be made. The first is designed to affect all the children (or, indeed, all the people) in the particular community concerned, so that it would be hoped to observe and measure an improvement in the juvenile delinquency rate of the community as a whole. The second would affect only selected children, such as those attending particular schools or those making use of a particular social service, and its success would be measured by observing the progress of the children affected in comparison with that of some comparable group of other children. So far, the first, more comprehensive type of study has presented such daunting technical, material and political difficulties that none has been attempted outside the United States. The difficulties of the second, more limited, kind of action study are still formidable in the realms of both theory and practice; but they are not so formidable as to stop these studies being attempted, and I hope we shall see a growing association between social action and research, the action being in some cases based on a specific research design and in other cases the research being no more than the observation and assessment of action which was being undertaken in any event.

2. Forensic science and the police and judicial systems

This brings me to the second of the three main groups into which I suggested criminological research might go.

Forensic science is concerned very largely with the examination and interpretation, using the ordinary methods of the physical sciences, of the material effects of crime; it is perhaps understandable that it is regarded as a highly specialized subject rather aside from the main stream of criminology. It is not, perhaps, so clear why research on police work has until a few years ago been so neglected in this country, as in most others. The actions and attitudes of the police are so much an integral part of the crime picture we see, and have so much to do with the painting of it, that one might expect such research to have had an early place in the time-table. Why it did not may be an interesting piece of history, but is not one that can be gone into now. But in recent years some studies of the police and the effect of police attitudes on some aspects of crime have been undertaken; and the Home Office now has its own Police Research and Planning Branch which is responsible for research on the operational work and the deployment of police along with the study of some highly technical matters such, for example, as the identification of fingerprints.

Research on the judicial system is again something that formerly, in Great Britain, received less than its share of attention from criminologists. The study of the aims of sentencing, and the utility of different kinds of sentence in relation to such aims, has begun only comparatively recently. The real nature of the phenomenon of general deterrence has only begun to be examined. But also the whole of our judicial process, and its relation to other possible systems, awaits more research; as do also the effects of different court systems on verdicts and sentences; the treatment of accused persons before conviction; the enforcement of orders to pay money; and so on, in a long list, down to perhaps the examination of court time-tables and appointment systems in order to seek to minimize the waste of every-one's time. Research methods on some of these questions may con-sist of standard social survey procedures, or other well-known techniques; but to deal with others it will be necessary to continue a process, already begun on a small scale, of working out methods on the spot in collaboration with the judicial system itself.

This is what my own research unit is trying to do at present in the Crawley juvenile court. The juvenile court magistrates are colla-borating with the police, the probation service, the education and children's services and ourselves

> to examine the social, educational and behavioural characteristics of juvenile offenders in comparison with those of other children;
> to study the sentencing process at the juvenile court;
> and to follow up the offenders and the control group in terms of reconviction, social and educational adjustment, and employ-ment history, until the end of the juvenile period.

This research goes beyond merely a study of the judicial process. But that is, nevertheless, an important part of it, and this is, I think, an excellent example of the kind of collaboration I have been speaking about.

3. *Sentencing and the treatment of offenders*

Lastly, I come to research on the treatment of offenders. This is a subject that has attracted more research effort than any other, par-ticularly in this country but also in most others. This may be partly because it seemed to offer a quicker pay-off than most other subjects (there are eminent criminologists even today who adopt a very dis-couraging tone towards research on causation and prevention); partly because the government was directly responsible for a large penal system which it knew to be, in some of its aspects, sadly out of date; but also, I think, partly for rather diverse reasons, relating to the individuals concerned, the teachers and associates who had influenced them, and the work done in the U.S.A.—particularly, perhaps, the earlier work by the Gluecks on the prediction of reconviction among prisoners.

There are two general aspects of research on treatment of offenders. First, from the point of view of a court, to the extent that it is looking for the sentence that will be most likely to stop a particular offender from offending again (short of life imprisonment), how to help it to find that sentence.

Secondly, from the point of view of the administrators of a particular kind of penal treatment, how to use this treatment to the best advantage in dealing with the offenders it has to deal with, and how it can improve the treatment.

Now a court has no power to alter existing forms of penal treatment or even to specify one prison or borstal or probation officer in preference to another. So looking at this from the court's point of view, we have simply a short list of penalties or orders—discharge, fine, probation and so on—and research workers have only to analyse the characteristics of offenders, of their offences or anything they think may be relevant, and see whether they can specify combinations or degrees of characteristics which give a clear indication (based on the history of people sentenced in the past) in favour of one sentence rather than another. A lot of work has been done on this and so far it is proving very difficult to find any way of obtaining indications that, for a particular offender, one sentence is likely to be more successful than another. It is found, so far, that the characteristics of an offender, of his offence and his criminal history are better predictors of the likelihood of reconviction than anything to do with the sentence he is given.

You may agree that it is against common sense to accept that penal treatment has no effect at all, good or bad, on most offenders (though we can admit that it has no effect on some). At least we shall need a lot more evidence before we believe anything of the kind. So we have to explore in two further directions. First, we may not yet have managed to discover those characteristics in an offender, if there are any, which interact with a particular kind of treatment; so we must make further analyses of offenders' characteristics. Secondly, we must remember that most forms of penal treatment—prison, borstal, probation, even fines—are heterogeneous. A particular offender might do well at one borstal but badly at another. If this were so, then, unless the allocation system were right, we might be allowing the bad results to cancel out the good; but a rearrangement of offenders within a particular system might produce a better result.

In order to get anywhere with this line of thought we need new and better ways of analysing offenders into types and groups and we need a great deal more progress in analysing and defining types of treatment.

Also, we need to develop studies of criteria of the success of treatment, remembering that it may possibly make little sense to think of a particular sentence followed by a limited follow-up period, but that rather it may be necessary to think in terms of the modification, over several years and perhaps several sentences, of a criminal career.

Quite a lot of research on the description and grouping of offenders has been and is being carried out but, so far, little has been done by way of scientific description of penal treatment in a way that would make it possible to define sensibly how the treatment in one place, or by one person, differs from that in another. In the probation research that we are doing in the Home Office we have made a start, but there is a long way still to go. And yet this problem—to define types of treatment and to define types of offender and to examine the interaction between offenders and treatments of the different types—is perhaps the central research problem in the field of the treatment of offenders, and we must put it down as one of the most important aims of this kind of research.

In trying to solve this problem, research will need a lot of co-operation from the treatment services concerned. There have constantly been innovations and changes within the penal system, and in order to make possible the evaluation of such changes they should as far as possible be systematized and carried out within research designs. In particular places this is already being done, and I hope eventually this will be the rule rather than the exception.

It is indeed true that not only in the field of the treatment of offenders but also in most of the other fields I mentioned—crime as a social phenomenon; the causation and prevention of crime; the police and judicial systems—progress will depend largely on the co-operation of the various authorities and administrations concerned and of the men and women who are working in the systems; in the courts, the prison service, the police, the schools, the child care services, the probation service, the youth service, the health services —and so on, with apologies to those I have omitted. Ultimately they can make or break research.

I believe that most of them are willing to co-operate. Many are eager to do so and are disposed to blame research for not going ahead more quickly. But the impediments are the shortage of first-class experienced research workers and the lack of time and machinery for communication between all those concerned so that a strategy for research and experiment can be worked out. These, however, are the ordinary problems of research administration in the criminological field, and I have no doubt that one of these days we shall overcome these obstacles and press on cheerfully towards the next. In the meantime I tender the thanks of all research workers to those who give them so much help, and offer also our gratitude, which Sir Robert Walpole defined as "a lively sense of *future* favours".

IV

RESEARCH PROBLEMS

7. THE NATURE OF CRIME

Mr. Lodge's three broad groups of research questions begin with inquiries into the nature of crime. Mr. N. Howard Avison's (I) paper on "Changing Patterns in Criminal Behaviour" belongs to this group.

During the last 40 years there has been, generally speaking, an almost continuous annual increase in the number of indictable offences known to the police. The rate of this increase has been far in excess of that of the population.

However, the distribution of offences committed, as represented by offence groups, has changed very little. Yet, within these groups of offences there have been changes in pattern. For example, it has been offences against property with violence (in which more than £100 has been stolen) that have increased most rapidly in recent years. A study of offences against property without violence also shows that the theft of valuable goods has been increasing more quickly than other kinds of stealing. The available evidence seems to indicate that the profession of crime pays rich dividends and that many more expert criminals are committing offences. A survey of the group of offences classified as "violence against the person" indicates that the increase in this group is mainly in malicious woundings, with a comparatively small increase in the more serious felonious woundings; by contrast, there was a decrease in non-indictable assaults. An alteration in police methods of recording might account for this; if this is so, it might reflect a decreased public tolerance of crimes of violence.

With regard to non-indictable offences, the overall pattern is not one of marked increase. Indeed, if traffic offences are excluded, the general trend seems to be downward. For certain offences, the decrease is due to new legislation: for example, betting and gaming offences and offences by prostitutes. Other non-indictable offences show only minor changes which, in comparison with the increase in indictable crime, is difficult to understand. However, there are some non-indictable offences that are increasing at least at the same rate as indictable crime. For example, offences of taking and driving away motor vehicles (and thefts of motor vehicles) have risen sharply. Drunkenness has increased sharply among young persons of both sexes and among young men. Addiction to certain drugs is becoming a noticeable problem in borstals and approved schools.

Although it is difficult to ascribe the increase in crime to any specific group, the growth of criminality among the young is clearly significant. The peak age for indictable crime, as has long been known, is 14. For non-indictable offences, excluding motoring offences, the peak occurs in the group aged 17 and under 21 (the statistics unfortunately do not give age-specific rates for non-indictable offences, but the trend is nevertheless clear). In 1965 a new feature appears for indictable offences: an additional peak at the age of 17. Furthermore, delinquency among the 15-year-olds has now increased to the level of that of the 13-year-olds. Previously, the age-specific crime rate had risen smoothly to 14, dropped steeply at 15, then followed a gentle curve through the years to adulthood. Now, with the increase in teenage criminality, there might be a trend towards higher crime rates among young adults which would smooth the curve, or might even lead to a more pronounced peak at the age of 17. When cautions are taken into account, the peak age group for those found guilty of non-indictable offences is less exaggerated than when cautions are omitted.

The increase in well-organized and lucrative crimes suggests the activity of a fairly small number of persistent professional criminals. Sometimes, when these offenders are detected and charged, allegations of intimidation of witnesses and of jurors suggest that even in custody such offenders could control or enjoy the protection of some organized groups prepared to interfere with the course of justice.

The number of crimes resulting from the activities of persistent career criminals is not ascertainable for certain. But it has been estimated that there are probably no more than two or three hundred criminal leaders and professional receivers. If it is assumed that each arranges crimes at the rate of one a fortnight (a fairly high rate) they would be responsible for less than 8000 principal crimes a year. However, one of the outstanding characteristics of the way in which organized criminals work is the large number of subsidiary crimes they commit, such as the theft of explosives, cutting equipment, cars and vans, and possibly even money for the payment of gang members to be recruited in the future.

Moreover, such criminals are prepared to commit crimes of violence, attacking security guards or night-watchmen, or members of the public, in order to ensure the success of their plans. Therefore, if every principal crime involved the commission of three subsidiary crimes, the total activity of these criminals would amount to 30,000 crimes annually (or about 3 per cent of the total). To dismiss activities in this group on the ground that 3 per cent seems low would be to miss the point; such criminals would plan to take property of considerable value. Accordingly, this rather small number of criminals might be responsible for the vast majority of the increasing number of crimes in which more than £100 is stolen. Professional criminalism could also be responsible for crimes which are rarely reported to the police: inter-gang violence is unlikely to be so reported unless someone dies. Estimates of the value of the property stolen vary, but it is unlikely to be less than £50 million annually. Overall, for indictable offences, the police detect fewer than 4 crimes in 10. With profits so high and risks so low, it is inevitable that a new class of professional criminal should emerge.

What about the other 97 per cent of crime? One of the most recent suggestions is that criminality in this country is much more widespread than is commonly believed. For conclusive evidence, we must await the findings of research in self-reported criminality. But if the American and Scandinavian experience is anything to go by, we may expect over 90 per cent of children and young people to admit committing at least one crime. This would confirm studies such as May's survey of a group of Liverpool children and would lend some support to the oft-quoted recent statistic that 29 per cent of males can be expected to be convicted of an indictable offence at some time of their lives.

However, calculations based on a single year of criminal statistics, at a time of rapidly increasing crime rate, must be viewed with caution. These calculations can mean no more than this: if age-specific crime rates do not change, then by the year 2033, 29 per cent of males will have been convicted at least once of an offence which we now call indictable. But estimates of the prevalence of criminality for all indictable offences are not very useful; they only provide an overall perspective. It would be of much greater value to assess the prevalence of criminality in relation to social and demographic factors. Unfortunately, the data on which such a study needs to be based are not, as yet, available. One also needs to be much more specific about offences. It is clear from Fig. 1 and Table 1 that marked differences between the different categories of offences exist. The figures are derived from the *Supplementary Criminal Statistics for 1963* and relate not only to indictable offences but also to those non-indictable offences which are included in the Home Office Standard List of Offences.

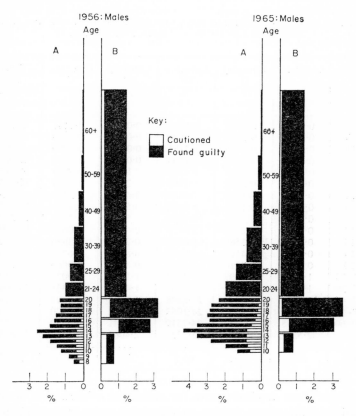

FIG. 1. Showing male offenders as a proportion of the population of their age or age group; 1956 and 1965. A, offenders found guilty of indictable offences, or cautioned by the police. B, offenders found guilty of non-indictable offences, or cautioned by the police (non-motoring).

Because these additional offences are included, the overall risk of being found guilty at least once in a lifetime rises, for males, to almost 39 per cent. As might be expected, category III offences against

F

property shows the highest prevalence, of 25 per cent. The miscellaneous category V is the next highest, with almost 7 per cent. Category I, offences of violence, and category IV, frauds and false pretences, and receiving stolen goods, are each about 2·5 per cent; while sexual offences, category II, is the smallest risk category, of under 2 per cent. The statistics on which these figures are based do

TABLE 1. CUMULATIVE RISK OF BEING CONVICTED FOR THE FIRST TIME OF A STANDARD LIST OFFENCE: MALES, 1963 (see Fig. 1)

Age	Category I %	Category II %	Category III %	Category IV %	Category V %	Total all categories %
8	0·0003	0·0000	0·1686	0·0036	0·0441	0·2166
9	0·0024	0·0009	0·5680	0·0128	0·1429	0·7269
10	0·0062	0·0033	1·2181	0·0424	0·2889	1·5590
11	0·0132	0·0090	2·1303	0·0873	0·4697	2·7096
12	0·0300	0·0209	3·4303	0·1693	0·6929	4·3435
13	0·0586	0·0492	5·1967	0·2973	0·9358	6·5376
14	0·1102	0·1000	7·3120	0·4352	1·2219	9·1793
15	0·1976	0·1618	9·0102	0·5287	1·4838	11·3821
16	0·3039	0·2333	10·4636	0·5964	1·7418	13·3390
17	0·4586	0·2941	12·0729	0·6762	2·0678	15·5697
18	0·6504	0·3563	13·5222	0·7493	2·3966	17·6747
19	0·8108	0·4167	14·6728	0·8102	2·6755	19·3860
20	0·9580	0·4710	15·6347	0·8746	2·9069	20·8451
21–25	1·4387	0·6899	18·4463	1·1354	3·9026	25·6129
25–30	1·8303	0·9581	20·5855	1·4006	4·5335	29·3080
30–40	2·2404	1·3258	22·8298	1·8233	5·3994	33·6187
40–50	2·4251	1·6057	24·1068	2·1342	6·0770	36·3487
50–60	2·5018	1·7753	24·7510	2·3041	6·3830	37·7151
60+	2·5502	1·9495	25·2238	2·4063	6·5498	38·6795
%	6·6	5·1	65·2	6·2	16·9	100·0

not give more detailed figures for individual offences, but in comparison with crimes known to the police, interesting differences emerge, which may be seen from Table 2.

From this it can be seen that offences of violence against the person and sexual offences, as well as the miscellaneous group of offences, show proportionately many fewer offences known compared with the risk of being convicted of these.

In almost all categories of crime and for all ages, first offenders outnumber recidivists. Only males aged 16 and over convicted of offences

TABLE 2. PROPORTIONS OF STANDARD LIST OFFENCES KNOWN TO THE POLICE
DIVIDED INTO FIVE CATEGORIES RELATED TO THE PROPORTIONAL RISK OF
BEING CONVICTED OR FOUND GUILTY FOR THE FIRST TIME OF SUCH AN
OFFENCE: MALE OFFENDERS, 1963

Type of offence		Offences known to the police	Proportional risk, first offender
Category I:	Violence against the person	2·5	6·6
Category II:	Sexual offences	2·2	5·1
Category III:	Offences against property	85·2	65·2
Category IV:	Frauds and false pretences	6·0	6·2
Category V:	Other standard list offences	4·1	16·9
Total: Per cent		100·0	100·0
Number[a]		1,069,388	128,407

[a] The number of standard list offences known to the police was estimated by summing indictable crimes known to the police with the numbers of persons proceeded against for non-indictable standard list offences.

in category III show a slight preponderance of recidivists. The proportion of first offenders is further increased if persons cautioned by the police as an alternative to taking proceedings in court are included; for persons cautioned may be regarded, for the most part, as first offenders.

Few statistics are available to confirm the general impression that juveniles band together more often and commit crimes. The only information regularly available is that contained in the annual report of the Commissioner of Police of the Metropolis, which shows that, of persons under 21 arrested for indictable offences, about 6 in 10 were operating with other persons. The size of the group was two or three in 9 out of 10 cases. These broad figures have remained largely unchanged for the last 10 years.

This does not mean that there has been no increase in juvenile criminal gangs—the low clear-up rate in the metropolis means that four out of five criminals are not detected. However, the argument that criminals must eventually become statistically unlucky enough to be detected applies equally to groups as to individuals. The true explanation probably lies in the fact that the Commissioner does not give details of persons arrested or summoned for non-indictable offences.

There may be many groups of juvenile offenders involved in malicious damage, taking and driving away motor-cars, and so forth, who would never appear in the annual report for the Metropolitan area. Dr. Downes, in his study *The Delinquent Solution*, suggests that there are no delinquent sub-cultures leading to definite gang formation. He states (p. 134):

> The main factor militating against the emergence of "criminal" sub-cultures in England is the relative absence of any demonstrably successful "illegitimate opportunity structure". There are no syndicated "rackets" in the American sense, and what pale imitations exist—in racing, dogtracks, "protection", and prostitution—are small and highly localized.

This may no longer be true. It seems that a "demonstrably successful" criminal class is emerging, and that if this is all that prevents juvenile gang formation, within the next 5 years an English Thrasher will have ample source material.

Dr. T. Willett's (XXIX) paper on "The Motoring Offender" takes the examination of the nature of crime into more detail. He starts with the hypothesis that driving a motor-car is a social activity in which attitudes towards others are reflected in the same way as they are in all other kinds of social activity, including criminality. Driving is not a unique kind of activity in which personality is irrelevant.

This hypothesis is decisive in answering the question: Are motoring offenders criminological phenomena, or are they more properly subjects for the traffic and automobile engineer to deal with? It may be that they are both, but the extent to which they fall in one category or the other is important.

It is only recently that the possibility has been considered that motoring offences and offenders might be explained in terms of social behaviour, for it has been traditional in the country to regard them as "different" from crime and criminals as they are usually conceived. In motoring cases, the offender is usually a faceless entity whose behaviour is discussed in terms of his personal competence as an operator of his vehicle. Medical or probation reports are hardly ever required by the court and evidence as to previous non-motoring convictions is often excluded as being irrelevant. Treatment tends to be rather mechanical, and rule-of-thumb tariff-type sentences are usual. In these cases, more than in any other kind, there is treatment without diagnosis, with its not surprising consequences of relapse.

It is, therefore, quite difficult to examine this hypothesis with confidence because the information about offenders as individuals is, as yet, so limited. There are, however, some clear indications that what is involved is by no means distinctive behaviour outside the ken of the criminologist. Certain factors influence this behaviour:

1. Social adjustment

Research evidence seems to suggest that serious motoring offenders tend to have criminal convictions, broken marriages, poor school records, unstable employment histories, and sometimes mental illness. Drunken drivers tend to include a high proportion of alcoholics, some of whom might use cars as instruments of violence. Cars are also used sometimes as a means of committing suicide by the mentally unstable.

2. Sex

There is some conflict of evidence here. Women drivers might have a slightly higher accident record, possibly due to relative lack of experience. But men greatly outnumber women as motoring offenders. In fact the male–female ratio in motoring offences is much as it is in other types of offences. Moreover, women very rarely commit more than one motoring offence. This may be related to the difference in masculine and feminine roles.

3. Age

Motoring offenders are mainly young—most of them are in their late teens or early twenties. There are very few over 45.

4. Occupation

Manual workers provide a high proportion of serious motoring offenders. Recent Californian research also shows the comparatively low occupational status of such offenders. There is no evidence of police bias against class—on the contrary, the police seem very fair. There is more evidence of lower intelligence among serious motoring offenders; and it may be that the higher intelligence required for good driving is more likely to be found in those of better education and in the non-manual occupational groups.

5. *Health*

There is some evidence of poor mental health but not yet sufficient data on physical health. Research into accident history shows this to be significantly related only to exposure to risk.

8. CAUSATION AND PREVENTION

Mr. Lodge's first group of research questions included not only the nature of crime but research into its causation and prevention. This is where Dr. Michael Rutter's (XXII) paper on "Sickness in Parents and Delinquency in the Children" is relevant.

The primary prevention of delinquency is hampered by an ignorance of which events or what situations are likely to lead to deviant behavioural development in the child. Chronic physical or mental illness in a parent, or the death of a parent, may be such events. The results of recent investigations show that for children in these families there may be a high risk of emotional and behavioural disorders, including delinquency.

The effects on the child of parental physical illness, of parental mental disorder, and of parental death, are examined in a study of nearly 1000 child patients attending the Maudsley Hospital. One in five of these children with psychiatric disorders had a parent who had been under psychiatric care or who had attempted or committed suicide—a rate three times as high as that in closely matched control groups of children attending dental or paediatric clinics. The difference cannot be explained in terms of a bias in referral. The association with disorder in the child is most marked where the parent has a personality disorder, or a chronic neurotic condition, when *both* parents have a mental disorder and when the parental symptoms directly involve the child.

The incidence of chronic or recurrent illness in the parents of Maudsley Hospital children was also significantly raised, being twice that in matched control groups. Again, referral biases cannot be invoked to account for the difference. There is a significant tendency for these chronic or recurrent illnesses to be associated with some degree of mental disorder; but the illnesses also have other impacts on family life.

The incidence of parental deaths was also increased, the number being double that expected on the basis of the Registrar-General's figures, controlled for age, sex, marital status and secular trends. Parental deaths are often followed by a variety of family disturbances, including the break-up of the family, morbid grief reactions in the spouse, remarriage of the surviving parent, etc. Paternal and maternal deaths are equally associated with psychiatric disorder in the child. The association between parental death and disorder in the child is strongest when the child was bereaved at the age of 3 or 4 years; but it is notable that immediate grief reactions are rarely the cause of psychiatric referral. The onset of disorder is often delayed many years, frequently until early adolescence, suggesting that factors consequent upon the death are as important as the death itself.

Parental illness is not associated with any specific behavioural syndrome in the children; but most of the disorders include anti-social behaviour and often there is frank delinquency. The lack of specificity in the type of disorder suggests the importance of the child's own characteristics—including his temperamental attributes.

There is no relationship between the form of the parental illness and the form of the disorder of the child. The sex of the ill (or dead) parent is, however, important. When mental illness occurs in the mother or when the mother dies, there is a particular association with psychiatric disorder in the daughter rather than the son, emphasizing the importance of the child's relationship with the same-sexed parent.

The association between parental mental illness and psychiatric disorder in the child is considered in terms of an environmental effect (see also Stern, 1948; Fabian and Donohue, 1956; Anthony, 1959; Ehrenwald, 1958; Huschka, 1941; Treudley, 1946; Main, 1958; Janet, 1925; Pollak, 1952; Ackerman, 1958; Morris, 1958).

Nevertheless, it is most important to examine whether or not the relationship between illness in parents and their children can be explained largely in genetic terms.

Certainly, there is evidence that genetic factors play a part in the development of child psychiatric disorder, but also that non-genetic factors probably play a more decisive role than in disorders which begin in adult life. However, what matters here is not whether genetic factors play a part in aetiology, but the more limited question of whether the genetic factors underlying *adult* psychiatric disorder are the same as those underlying psychiatric disorders in *childhood*.

An opportunity to examine this question was provided by the fact that a number of children had both a natural parent and a step-parent and that either the natural parent or step-parent had had a mental illness. When comparable situations were examined, illness occurred in the step-parent almost, but not quite, as often as in the natural parent (six times as compared with ten times). This suggests that genetic influences are probably not of major importance in the association.

This conclusion was supported by circumstantial evidence from other parts of the investigation. Genetic factors can scarcely be invoked to account for the relationship between parental physical illness and disorder in the child. The effects of physical and mental illness showed some differences but to the extent that they were similar they provide indirect evidence that non-genetic factors may have been relevant in the association with mental illness as well as with physical illness in the parent.

The lack of relationship between the type of parental disorder and the type of disorder in the child also argues strongly against a genetic link, as does the very heterogeneity of disorders found in association with parental illness. Stronger evidence in favour of an environmental effect is the finding that direct involvement of the child in the symptoms of the parental illness was more important than the form that the parental disorder took. In some cases, the disorders in parent and child were related in time. Often the child and parent tended to relapse together or improve together. In many more it was found that the child did not improve until he was placed away from home—such as in a boarding school. Children with mentally ill parents were twice as likely as other children attending the same clinic to be placed away from their parents. So, whatever caused the disorder in the child, the presence of an ill parent seems to be important in its continuation.

If the association between illnesses in parents and psychiatric disorder in their children is not primarily due to a genetic link, what is the mechanism of the interaction? Further studies are required before this question can be answered satisfactorily, but it is clear that parental illness is often associated with disturbances in the home and in the family, and it is probable that these contribute towards the development of the child's disorder.

Parental mental disorder is most likely to be followed by behavioural disturbance in the children when the parents exhibit long-standing abnormalities of personality. The "seriousness" of the illness in terms of neurosis or psychosis is probably not important, but the involvement of the child in the symptoms of the illness does seem to be crucial.

The adjustment of families may also be more difficult when the patient's disorder is not recognized as an illness. The spouse and the children may be able to make allowances and adjust when they perceive the patient's peculiar behaviour as due to illness. Such adjustments are more difficult when his irritability, moodiness, or hostility are seen as the normal feelings of a parent who has inexplicably turned against them.

The affectional bond between parent and child seems to be adversely affected particularly when the illness is chronic and when hostility to the child (a not infrequent occurrence in neurotic or depressive illnesses) is present. When this happens the child often suffers, but it seems that the deleterious effect may be mitigated by a good relationship with the other parent.

To a large extent the presence of one parent who has a good relationship with the child can make up for the absence or deviant behaviour of the other, whether a mother or a father. On the other hand, in that the child of the same sex as the ill parent is especially liable to develop disorder, the relationship with the same sexed parent does seem to have an added importance.

Children in families where *both* parents are ill or where the parental illness is accompanied by the break-up of the marriage seem to be especially at risk. Continuing contact with a mentally ill parent might be harmful for the child if the illness disrupts family life. On the other hand, contact with even a severely ill parent may still be beneficial, so long as the illness does not seriously impair affectional relationship within the home.

Clearly, some illnesses are more socially disruptive than others, but the effect of illness upon the health of other members of the family is probably related more to the impact on family life than the clinical symptoms. Though the social disturbance associated with psychosis is well recognized, the disturbance accompanying chronic neurosis may be more severe, if less flamboyant; and the social consequences of chronic illness—though they may be milder—are often very similar.

In his paper on "Deprived Children and their Families", Dr. Schaffer (XXIV)* illustrates the need to see prevention in a wider

* Reproduced in full in the *Howard Journal of Penology and Crime Prevention* *12* (2), 1967.

framework than that of the prevention of crime. Social pathology takes many forms, of which crime, though the most thoroughly studied, is but one. The study of various forms of social pathology should not be kept in rigidly separated categories since both methodological and substantive findings in one area can enlighten work in another. Deprivation is a form of social pathology in its own right. In the past, deprivation and crime have generally been discussed in terms of a possible causal relationship, but Dr. Schaffer's approach is to treat both phenomena as manifestations of possibly similar social structures. His research project, investigating the reasons for bringing a child into the care of the local authority, focuses on one particular situation which frequently results in children having to be taken into care: when a mother has to go into hospital for another confinement. In one year, 14 per cent of all admissions to care in Scotland result from this circumstance. The research attempts to ascertain why, in face of this particular crisis, some families must seek public help or risk disintegration, whilst others can cope from their own resources. By comparing families who send their children into care with matching families confronted by the same crisis, who make their own private arrangements, it becomes possible to examine various hypotheses about the reasons for family strength and independence, and to isolate the factors responsible for inadequacy in this situation.

Methodologically, this research presents problems frequently encountered in criminological research—the fallibility of available statistics, the problem of multiple causation, and the alternation between psychological and sociological explanation. Also in common is the question of the conditions of family life which give rise to social problems. Each of the children taken into care could be said to represent an instance of family inadequacy. The data obtained show that the families which were able to cope with the mother's absence differed as a group from those whose children went into care in the quality of their interpersonal relationships and in the internal cohesiveness of the family group. This difference is illustrated with reference to such variables as the attitudes of fathers towards helping in the home, and the links maintained by the family with the grandparents. The contacts between the families and the community, including social agencies, is also examined.

The minor crisis represented by a mother's confinement can bring to light many families which are liable to social breakdown, and such an event can provide an opportunity for preventive action by social workers. At the same time, it is possible that some children are accepted into care too easily in such circumstances. The resources of a family may sometimes not be utilized if local authority care presents an easy solution to the crisis. There is perhaps a danger that taking a child into care may sometimes weaken a family's capacity to cope with similar crises in future. There is generally a greater potential for growth in responsibility and self-confidence if a person is helped to deal with a problem and not merely relieved of it.

9. TREATMENT RESEARCH

The only example of Mr. Lodge's third group of research questions —those concerning the sentencing and treatment of offenders—is the paper by Dr. Steven Folkard (XIII) on "Probation—Techniques and Results".

A treatment classification system was developed by the Probation Research section of the Home Office Research Unit which took account of varying amounts of support and control, and the use of individual and situational methods. Preliminary findings from a pilot study in Middlesex suggest that those probationers who complete their period on probation in a satisfactory way have received less control than those who fail. Further research would be necessary to show whether these results were due to the treatment given or in spite of it.

It seems likely that outcome is determined by interaction between the type of offender and the type of treatment, and that there is no one particular type of treatment which is the most effective for all types of offender. A classification for all types of offenders was developed which took account of personality problems and social problems. The probationer's personality was assessed as inadequate, disturbed or normal, and his social situation as delinquent, stressful or normal.

In one probation area a matching experiment is being carried out in which, using the classification of offenders and of treatment, an attempt is being made to allocate probationers to those officers who are considered most capable of providing the type of treatment which seems to be needed in each case. Efforts will be made to show whether this produces better results than the more usual geographical allocation.

Probationers are not merely the passive recipients of things which are done to or from them. Treatment is essentially mediated through a personal relationship between the probation officer and the probationer, within which there are a series of social stimuli, response and counter-response. The concept of relationship is emphasized in casework theory, and many probation officers would claim that the results of treatment depend upon the nature and quality of the relationships which are established between officers and probationers.

Part of the probation research consists of a systematic study of these relationships in which special attention is being paid to social interaction and to interpersonal perception. The aim of the study of social interaction is to examine, categorize and analyse what happens in the probation interview. The methods of study made use of Resource Process Analysis as developed by Richard Longabaugh.

This method enables a detailed analysis to be made of the form and content of social interaction, and seems to be particularly appropriate to the study of the kinds of interview which take place in probation.

The main sample, which is a voluntary one, is being collected by probation officers in the Birmingham Probation Area, who are tape-recording interviews with male probationers, aged 17 and under 21. It is hoped to obtain sixty interviews in all, and that of this total half will consist of "continuous treatment". Five probation officers have been asked each to tape-record six consecutive interviews with one probationer. It is also hoped to have half the sample, i.e. thirty probationers, in the study of interpersonal perceptions, in order to link the two theoretical aspects of the treatment relationship. Some of them have also been included in the study of interaction of types of treatment and types of offender. The length of the interviews ranges between 4 minutes and 50 minutes, with the majority being under 15 minutes long. Analysis will attempt to show the relative occurrence of different kinds of interaction, and to develop indexes of successful support, successful control and successful interpretation.

The use of a tape-recorder has limitations but it seemed to be the most useful method available. Its influence on the interviews soon diminished in most cases, and though it only records verbal behaviour, the verbal exchange is one of the most important parts of an interview.

The study of interpersonal perception is concerned with describing the probation officer's and the probationer's perception of (1) the relationship between them; (2) the aims, methods and effectiveness of probation; and (3) the probation officer's role. Twenty probation officers and 120 male probationers aged 17 and under 21 (from Coventry, Birmingham and Glasgow) are being interviewed, using a schedule which has been developed for this purpose. Many of the questions are designed to link up with those being used in the study of social interaction.

From the analysis of the data an attempt will be made to show the ways in which officers and probationers perceive each other, whether perceived relationships vary with type of probationer and type of officer, and whether they are associated with the success and failure of cases.

The sample of probationers studied will not be a representative one, but the primary task, in the first instance, is to identify the most relevant treatment variables, and to develop valid and reliable methods for studying them. Before it is possible to say certain things about probation techniques, it is necessary to have the appropriate research techniques with which to describe them.

Probation officers are social workers concerned with the well-being of individual probationers, but they are also agents of a system concerned with the protection of society. Casework theory emphasizes the importance of giving the client support, and helping him to understand himself. A study of probation techniques must take account also of the attempts to control probationers and the use of situational methods.

Little is known about the relative effectiveness of different probation techniques. Nothing is known about how far a given outcome might have been achieved with different treatment or no treatment at all. So far neither statistical nor clinical methods have provided the tools with which to assess the effectiveness of treatment. Further progress would seem to depend on the development of more valid research techniques for classifying offenders, classifying treatment and measuring results.

THIRD KEYNOTE LECTURE

V

INDIVIDUALIZATION AND INVOLVEMENT IN TREATMENT AND PREVENTION

R. L. MORRISON (XX)

THE CLASSICAL DOCTRINE OF "INDIVIDUALIZATION"

The term "individualization" as applied to sentencing and treatment is one of the most overworked words in the whole business of dealing with offenders. No doubt it has served as a useful slogan in reminding the court that the offender requires as much attention as the offence. No doubt it has also had liberalizing and humanizing effects on institutional policy and practice, even allowing for the massive gap which normally lies between these two things. But as a guiding principle for the theory and practice of penology it has proved to be of very mixed value indeed. Having asserted this heretical position, let us examine it further.*

The late Sir Lionel Fox[1] commented on the "individualization of treatment" as follows: "I should not like too much to be read into this phrase. It does not mean that a special personal programme is prepared for each offender adapted to his particular needs in the light of a scientific diagnosis. It simply means that he gets what is most suitable for him of what the prison has to offer." At the same time, he did go on to refer to "the true basis of prison training" as consisting of "continuous personal attention from a staff whose duty it is to help him to adapt himself to prison life, to plan constructively for his future and to fit himself for that future". These comments perhaps understate the theory of *the programme approach* in prison

* The argument which follows is developed mainly in terms of prisons. Most of the points made have to be qualified, more or less, in applying them to other types of institutions (borstals, approved schools, etc.), but this does not mean to say that they can be qualified entirely out of existence.

training; they most certainly overstate the amount of *individual attention* given to prisoners and its relevance for their rehabilitation. But these are certainly the traditional components of individualized treatment which we have tended to equate, in much too facile a fashion, with social rehabilitation.

Clearly, one of the weaknesses of "*individual attention*" as a treatment principle is that this by itself provides no clues as to the precise nature or quality of the relationship required to change the offender. It is also clear that simply to insist on the uniqueness or idiosyncrasy of the individual case prevents the development of any rational system of diagnosis and treatment since this inevitably depends on some process of classifying and generalizing. Nor has the practice of formal psychotherapy or case-work contributed very much to general penological theory since these techniques are seldom sufficiently available or relevant for more than a minority of cases.

The programme approach has also been criticized on a variety of grounds. It is suggested that programmes of trade training or education or leisure activities have been more often used as control devices than as treatment instruments, that they are adjuncts or supplements to treatment rather than components of treatment. These unqualified assertions can be challenged, but the underlying argument is more subtle and telling—programmes are too often used as a means of avoiding the real problems of defective social attitudes or perceptions or relationships which land the majority of offenders in trouble with the law. According to this position, problem solving must precede programmes and programmes are useful only when they are relevant to problem-solving.[2]

An even more devastating blow to the traditional principles of individualized treatment has come, mainly but not entirely, from sociological studies of the organization, social systems and cultures of penal institutions.[3] The argument here, which has most relevance for large maximum-security establishments, runs as follows.

Certain criminogenic processes are generated or intensified in the prison situation as a response to excessive deprivation or over-repressive methods of control; other criminogenic or potential criminogenic factors are *inherent* in the very nature of imprisonment itself and cannot be eliminated merely by reducing the restrictions of prison life or relaxing oppressive methods of discipline.

In assessing these criminogenic aspects of imprisonment it is necessary to consider not only the nature of the personalities involved or the characteristics of prisons as social organizations and systems, but also the fact that penal institutions in general may be regarded as still in a state of transition between traditional punitive/custodial functions and those of treatment and rehabilitation. Finally, there remains the inescapable fact that any method of dealing with offenders by removing them from society inevitably creates problems as to how these offenders are to be reintegrated back into society on their release.

There is general agreement as to the existence, especially in large maximum-security institutions, of two separate but closely related social systems, that of the administration and that of the inmates. The inmate sub-culture is dominated by values and norms which are, for the most part, anti-social and anti-administration, and it is claimed that the main influence operating on the individual offender is the negative or criminogenic impact of inmate social life.

The "we–they" situation where staff and inmate systems in penal institutions are more or less in opposition is further complicated by the division between "custodial" and "treatment" functions within the staff group itself. Conflicts and contradictions in staff roles and rivalries between different types of staff reduce the effectiveness of any treatment approach. Further, such a situation may be exploited by inmates who are then able to resist treatment by manipulating staff and playing one member off against another.

The phrase "re-socialization within walls"[4] expresses the central paradox of traditional prison methods—the attempt to train or prepare offenders for freedom under conditions of captivity, in a controlled, artificial community which provides offenders with limited opportunities for acquiring the work skills and habits, or for developing and independently testing out the sense of social responsibility which they will need if they are not to resort to crime on their release. This dilemma is sharpened by the very fact of removing the offender from society, by disrupting and even destroying whatever slender family and other social supports he may have had, by creating problems of finding and settling to work or adjusting to new living situations on discharge. This becomes a vicious circle in the case of the offender who has been institutionalized for long periods, in that the longer he is cut off from society the greater become such obstacles to his resettlement and the more confinement has rendered him incapable of coping with his problems.

The traditional prison has thus come to be recognized as a small society excessively isolated from the larger society, a split community of inmates and staff, each group more or less divided among themselves. Against this kind of background it is not difficult to see how our traditional preoccupations with individual treatment methods and training programmes within the institution has not proved to be very fruitful in terms of results. However, we are coming to see certain things more clearly:

(i) Concentration of attention on the individual offender has proved to be somewhat sterile as a means of contributing to the construction of explanatory criminological theory. This is true whether we are interested in a highly abstract, organizing theory of criminality or in "theories of the middle range" specific to particular forms of deviant conduct.

As a further consequence of this, we have made little progress in evolving what Conrad has recently called "an internally consistent theory" of treatment, i.e. "a set of logically related principles based on empirically verified propositions" which would "account for the behaviour of the correctional client, prescribe a regime by which he can be restored to function in society, and account for the efficacy of the regime".[5]

That we are now trying to make up for lost time is evident from the amount of thinking which is now going into the production of typologies[6] and the search for "classifications that are related to treatment alternatives".[7] It is now becoming almost fashionable to attempt to develop a rationale for treatment on the basis of some explanatory or causal theory.

(ii) We have been diverted to a narrow treatment approach, focusing on the individual at the expense of what Sutherland called "the situation".* We have tended to concentrate our attention on the process of changing or treating the offender on the basis of immediate individual relationships, while largely ignoring the institutional social context within which treatment takes place and the still wider social context to which the offender will be released.

* It is a chastening experience to discover how much of the present argument was anticipated by Sutherland[8] writing in 1937 as follows: ". . . from the therapeutic point of view, attempts to change individuals one at a time while their groups and their culture remain unchanged is generally futile." ". . . you cannot have great success in altering persons by direct methods, and (that) you have a much better prospect of success by altering situations. We cannot reform prisoners in a prison community one at a time. Those who are interested in the program of

CHANGING ATTITUDES TO INSTITUTIONAL TREATMENT

There are, however, signs that we are radically revising our approach to the use of institutional measures and re-examining the proper place and scope for these as a means of protecting society and restoring offenders successfully to the community. This Congress has already learned that, in future, official policy and planning will seek to ensure that imprisonment will be used in a much more restricted and discriminating fashion, and the traditional prison will be modified and diversified in order to deal more effectively with the problems presented by different types of offender. In many ways, existing practice is already tending towards a reduction of some of the criminogenic factors of prison life and of the isolation of the institution from the outside community. All this can be taken as read.

At the same time we are beginning to look more closely at what institutional treatment ought to involve. This will become increasingly vital in the future as our new penal policy gets under way. The restricted use of the traditional prison will inevitably leave such institutions with a residual population whose treatment problems will be, on the whole, more severe than is the case at present and which will contain a higher proportion of offenders—professional criminals, dangerous, disturbed personalities, and so on—who must, in the present state of our knowledge and skills, be regarded as poor treatment prospects. For those who are treatable, a rational parole system implies that release will be timed to coincide with the offender's peak of readiness for return to the community. These new policies will be unsuccessful without a much more purposeful development of treatment techniques focused on the problems, attitudes, conditions and

---

individualization must take the prison community into account and not continue to talk and act as though the individual prisoner lived in a vacuum." ". . . community methods should be developed. This will mean a greater development of group work than is contemplated in the programs of individualization. It will mean community organization in which the prisoners themselves, at least in limited ways, participate. It will mean a closer integration of the general administration and the professional group." ". . . I have in mind a policy of individualization which will not regard the prisoner as an individual in a vacuum. It will be a socialized individualization rather than an individualistic individualization. It will be individualization integrated with a general program of community treatment."

circumstances of the offender which seem likely to produce further criminal behaviour in the future, irrespective of whether these problems contributed to his criminality in the past.*

Current thinking, then, would appear to be moving towards:

(i) Definitions of penological objectives in specific terms (such as individual "problem-solving"), the problems and their solutions being seen not merely in terms of criminality but also in relation to wider social values.

(ii) Definitions of the nature and processes of treatment (and, in particular, institutional treatment) in terms of its social context, i.e. a recognition that traditional techniques must be adapted and new techniques devised which will come to terms with, and somehow make constructive use of, the negative social setting within which they have to be applied.†

---

* I would go beyond this and suggest that the objectives of treatment will come to be defined more and more broadly in relation to the offender's optimum personal and social adjustment, his fullest self-realization and his potential contribution to the well-being and improvement of society itself. Despite the principle of lesser eligibility, training has always been related, to some extent, to this wider perspective. The approach to the offender in terms of education and vocational training programmes, for example, has been defended from time to time in just such terms. This has lent support to criticism of the programme approach as a frame without a picture, a concern with refinements at the expense of essentials. There are signs that a better balance will be achieved in future. It seems likely that in most cases we shall come to focus on the potential, future criminality of the offender as a central problem in his successful restoration to society, if by no means the whole problem.

† The conclusion to be drawn is not that, in the course of all this, the principle of "individualization" will be abandoned—rather that it will be applied in a more sensitive and more effective fashion. Nor does a typological approach necessarily imply that in deciding on treatment due recognition will not be given to the idiosyncrasies of the individual case. Gibbons[3] points out that "the diagnostician should be concerned *both* with the assignment of the problem to a set of general types *and* with the discovery of the unique features of a specific instance of problem behaviour. He must be sensitive both to the similarity of the case to others and to its unique features." It is by assessing the importance of these "unique features" in relation to the common factors operating, that the stock prescription is refined and modified as necessary to fit the individual case. Finally, the group approach to treatment in no way implies that the needs of the individual will be submerged. Thus, Polsky's study of the inmate social system in "Cottage Six" brought home to him the futility of using traditional therapeutic methods which were divorced from the boys' everyday life. He then suggested, not that individual treatment by clinical specialists should be abandoned, but that one should "change the basic unit of treatment from the individual boy to the entire Cottage and move the clinic into it. This changes the emphasis of treatment from rehabilitating youngsters to treating the Cottage culture, and the individual

It would be inappropriate to attempt to launch forth now on a systematic, detailed survey of all these new treatment developments. It is proposed instead to select for attention a few growing points which seem to be of some significance.

For some time now we have been looking more and more closely at the institution itself as a social setting within which treatment (more or less traditionally conceived) takes place. A more radical approach is now developing towards the institutional situation as not merely the context but the core of treatment. These trends are complementary rather than conflicting; they differ in emphasis rather than anything else.

TREATMENT IN TERMS OF THE INSTITUTIONAL "MILIEU"

Terms such as "milieu therapy" or "milieu management" are now fairly common currency. The words may still mean slightly different things to different people, but, in general, they refer to the possibilities of treating patients through a deliberate and systematic use of the institutional environment (in both its physical and social aspects), through "the planned management of the structure and processes of the situations in which they live". This approach is frequently presented as an overdue recognition of the limitations of what can be expected from individual or "clinical" procedures as traditionally applied in institutions. But there would still appear to be a wide range of opinion about what the notion of the "therapeutic milieu" involves.

(i) At one extreme the institutional environment is regarded as merely a background situation which may be exploited in order to facilitate and support (or at least not interfere with) traditional treatment techniques. Two complementary approaches are involved here—the treatment of the individual has to be based on a sensitive appreciation of his social life in the institution and related directly to this; the wider social processes occurring in the institution have to be structured and controlled in such a way as to support or absorb whatever treatment techniques

---

within the social life process of all his peers." He then went on to ask, "Does this violate the principle of individualization of treatment? On the contrary, it should increase the efficacy of psychotherapy because it will now mean treating the individual in his total life experience in the Cottage and institution."[9]

are used at the individual level. This is the variety of "milieu therapy" commonly advocated by clinicians.*

(ii) At the other extreme the social milieu is regarded as a powerful therapeutic influence in its own right, capable of operating independently of traditional treatment methods and even of replacing these. This position leads directly to the more rigorous forms of "community therapy".

The general trend, however, is to avoid extreme positions, to emphasize the importance of co-ordinating and integrating the whole range of treatment resources available within the institution, but to stress at the same time the need for individual and situational– environmental treatments to be balanced and interwoven together in whatever way seems most likely to meet the needs of the particular patients concerned. Exactly how is this to be done? When, or for what types of cases, should the relative emphasis be placed on en- vironmental or on individual factors in treatment? How far can the milieu be used as a support for clinical treatments and also as a therapeutic influence in its own right? Is it possible to maximize both uses of the milieu at the same time without becoming inconsistent? These are open and complicated questions, to be answered not on the basis of professional bias or preference, but by means of systematic empirical research into which particular patterns or combinations of treatment method will prove most effective for different types of cases. To test even the simplest treatment hypothesis of this kind will take some time. To build tested hypotheses into a rigorous treatment theory will take a very long time.

THE THERAPEUTIC COMMUNITY

There is, however, an increasing tendency to think in terms of "institutional treatment" as a whole. Prominent here is the notion of the "therapeutic community", which first emerged and developed in

* For a most persuasive statement of this point of view see Goldsmith, Schulman and Grossbard, from whom the following quotations are typical: "One cannot integrate a clinical process with an environment which is alien to it; which relies only on a rational approach taking behaviour at its face value. Nor is a benign environment consisting of warmth and love with good people and nutritive experiences sufficient to be integrated into a unified treatment plan". "Translation of the clinical process into all areas implies consistency and discretion emanating from a central source. The source obviously must be the clinician."[10]

its classical form as a contribution to the psychological treatment of certain types of neurotic illness and maladjustment.[11] There is considerable interest in the question of how far rigorous techniques of community therapy or the therapeutic community approach in more general and diluted forms can usefully serve as models for the treatment of offenders and disturbed anti-social persons.[12]

What essentially does the therapeutic community involve? In general, and at the risk of over-simplifying the position, community therapy can be regarded as a special form of milieu therapy where the main emphasis is placed on the therapeutic potentialities of the system of social relationships operating within the institution. This is a very general principle which, in practice, is applied in various ways, the "community" elements being given different degrees of prominence in different schemes of treatment.

The essential features of the system in its classical form as applied, for example, at the Henderson Hospital can be summed up as follows: the self-conscious pooling of all the resources of staff and patients alike in furthering treatment, the active involvement of patients in treatment roles; a democratic, egalitarian social structure, a sharing of responsibility and decision-taking, a permissive atmosphere, open communications (with no communications automatically regarded as privileged) and free expression of feelings; the provision of peer-group support to enable the patient to examine his poor relationships with others, to recognize and work through his difficulties with authority, to face up to the social consequences of his behaviour, to accept his need for personality and attitude change.

On the face of it, community methods of this kind have obvious attractiveness for dealing with the kinds of problems which arise in the penal treatment situation, obvious relevance for dealing with the unwilling patient who has suspicions or resentments of authority; for either neutralizing or exploiting the inmate culture; for the training and support of staff by developing methods of team work and so on.

Community therapy in its classical form is perhaps too unrealistic a model for the penal institution which is expected to contain and control its inmates as well as treat them. Such techniques perhaps constitute too big a challenge and too big a threat to established authoritarian methods of discipline, communications and decision-taking and to the established roles of specialist and non-specialist staff alike.

But broader and more flexible views are developing on how community therapy can be adapted to fit the needs of different kinds of patient or inmate and to meet, at the same time, the requirements and limitations of different kinds of treatment setting, without losing its essential character. Already, what can at least be regarded as a therapeutic community approach has been successfully introduced into such institutions, for example, as the psychiatric prison at Grendon Underwood[13] or a small hostel for homeless ex-Borstal lads.[14]

GROUP COUNSELLING AND ITS IMPLICATIONS

Attempts to achieve massive change in the treatment institution are relatively rare. Tactics of piecemeal change are much more common but these, not infrequently, turn out to have unforeseen consequences and repercussions throughout the total institutional situation. Group counselling conducted by basic grade custodial staff is probably the best current example of this kind of treatment innovation.[15] It becomes almost impossible, once counselling has genuinely got under way, to seal it off from other institutional activities and avoid facing up to its "community" implications.

It will be a long time before the group techniques themselves or our methods of evaluation are sufficiently refined to permit a rigorous demonstration that counselling produces in inmates sufficient levels of insight and control to effect a significant improvement in their social adjustment on release. But there is little doubt as to the beneficial short-term effects of counselling in the form of a more relaxed institutional climate, a reduction of tension between inmate and staff groups and so on.[16] At present in this country the tendency is to try to stabilize the position at this level in order to allow staff groups themselves to concentrate their attention on modifying the institutional system of communications, control and management in such a way as to achieve the kind of "complete and conflict-free synthesis of traditional and rehabilitative control systems" regarded as essential if the institution is ever to function in truly rehabilitative fashion.[17]

THE CHANGING ROLES OF INSTITUTIONAL STAFF

As an immediate consequence of these new approaches to institutional treatment, the traditional roles of staff undergo changes and complications. In the therapeutic community, the psychiatrist, for example, becomes involved in real life situations ("real", that is, in relation to the immediate social life of the institution). He can no longer act as the neutral or supportive therapist all of the time. On some occasions he may have to take restrictive action, on others he may have to remain unusually passive and non-interfering. Similar problems of role-change, role-overlap and role-conflict arise for other staff as well as for so-called "specialists".

Group counselling, also, not only involves the basic grade, non-specialist, staff in reconciling custodial and treatment roles, but generates pressure on such specialists as psychiatrists and psychologists to supplement or change their traditional treatment roles and function in a more extensive fashion, providing consultation, training and support for staff and working more closely with administrators in the area of institutional decision-taking.[18] This shift towards a more extensive functioning is not peculiar to specialists working in institutions but can be seen generally in the developing practice of social medicine, social psychiatry and psychology. There would seem to be little point in speculating as to whether such specialists were more influenced by institutional developments taking place around them—or vice versa.

THE STRATEGY OF INVOLVEMENT

Many of the trends we have been considering here can be drawn together in terms of old treatment principles which are now finding new forms of expression and application. One such principle is that of "involvement" in the treatment process. It has always been part of the rationale of treatment that the therapist was unlikely to be able to solve the patient's problem unless the latter was involved, motivated, willing, anxious and so on. What would seem to be new in the current version of involvement are definitions of the therapist, patient, problems, objectives and processes of treatment in wider and more complex terms. For example, we may imagine a rationale for community treatment being presented to the offender something like this:

"Your criminal behaviour is your problem and the problem of all the staff of the institution. The groups you belong to here and the community as a whole are also concerned with your criminality as part of their problem. Finally, your criminality is also society's problem, not only because it constitutes a threat to it but also because the responsibility for it must be accepted by society as well as by you."

This formulation blurs distinctions between patient and therapist, between individuals and their social groups, and society. It defines the problem as existing and the treatment process as occurring in different contexts within and around the individual at the same time. Others may wish to dismiss this as a muddled and dangerous form of double-talk but it can be defended as a serious attempt to illustrate some of the complexities which arise when we try to make sense of what is probably a prevailing trend in the evolution of our penal institutional treatment methods.

For there would seem to be obvious sense in confronting the prison community with the central task of solving the problem of its own criminality and of accepting responsibility for it in the same way as the hospital therapeutic community is asked to accept responsibility for its own mental health. It would seem sensible to try to feed back continuously to the whole institutional community information on how effectively it was achieving these aims. The most dramatic way to do this would be to return to the institution its own "failures", to force it to consume its own smoke. This is a strategy which, for several reasons, has up till now been capable of minimal application. The introduction of parole will bring it into the realm of the possible. The reverse technique would be to devise methods of involving the institution's "successes" and it would not seem too difficult to work out useful roles for such reformed offenders in the resettlement of others.

It is easy to over-play the difficulties of getting unco-operative prisoners, reluctant custodial officers, ex-offenders or apathetic members of the public actively involved in treatment and rehabilitation. In practice, the problem appears easier to solve than one would imagine. Experience suggests that even marginal or reluctant participation is enough in the first instance since the individual then tends to be carried along, despite himself, to the point where he has become fully involved. It would appear that this involvement occurs either as a result of powerful group pressures or simply through the continuance of the activity itself. There is reasonable evidence, for example, that custodial staff develop increasingly favourable pro-treatment attitudes simply by continuing to operate as group counsellors.[19]

A variety of theoretical formulations can be used to clarify some of the confusion which appears to underlie the kinds of approach which we are discussing. One example would be the principle of "retroflexive reformation" which Cressey[20] has expressed as follows:

The most effective mechanism for exerting group pressure (on members) will be found in groups so organized that criminals are induced to join with non-criminals for the purpose of changing other criminals. A group in which criminal A joins with some non-criminals to change criminal B is probably most effective in changing criminal A, not B.

Cressey points out that techniques of using criminals to change other criminals can be looked at in two ways. In the first approach a criminal-turned-reformer is viewed as the *agent* of change. He regards this approach as one in which the person to be changed can more easily achieve rapport and identification with the criminal-turned-reformer than with the professional reformer or the conventional law-abiding citizen.

Even more important is the second approach where the criminal "rehabilitator" remains himself the *target* of change. In his attempts to change criminals he must automatically identify himself with others engaged in reformation and in this way he continually reinforces not only non-criminal but also anti-criminal attitudes and values in himself.

Finally, Cressey puts forward the hypothesis that

> such success as has been experienced by Alcoholics Anonymous, Synanon, and even "official" programmes like institutional group therapy and group counselling, is attributable to the fact that such programmes require the reformee to perform the role of the reformer, thus enabling him to gain experience in the role which the group has identified as desirable.* [21]

A recent conference in California was devoted to the theme of "The involvement of those who are the products of a social problem in efforts to solve the problem". An astonishing variety of activities was discussed. In some of these involvement was secured on a purely voluntary basis, in others either token or realistic payment was made. These methods included the use of inmates as "social therapists", researchers, teachers, instructors and so on in penal institutions, or as community workers in crime prevention, the paid employment of juvenile gang leaders and members as field advisers and consultants to assist detached social workers in the reduction of gang warfare through the organization of more constructive leisure activities. Further illustrations were provided from the field of youth employment, education, mental health and so on.† [23]

* The same general idea has been expressed elsewhere as "the helper therapy principle" in this way: "We help others best when we ourselves are helped by trying to help." [22]

† Similar examples can be found in this country especially in the field of voluntary aftercare where several imaginative schemes for social clubs and group work with ex-prisoners have been started. There is obviously great scope for similar projects in the area of official aftercare and parole supervision.

It is not difficult to find other American examples of treatment and prevention projects which stress the importance of securing the maximum involvement of all sections of the community including its problem elements. Mobilization for Youth[24] and Harlem Youth Opportunities Unlimited[25] are typical of multiple, community-based action projects inspired by the President's Committee and the Juvenile Delinquent Act of 1961. Such schemes are nourished by Mertonian theories of anomie and the opportunity theories of Cloward and Ohlin.[26] Such preventive programmes are now being overtaken by those of the War on Poverty under the Economic Opportunity Act of 1964. In line with these developments is a recent American volume entitled *New Careers for the Poor*. This stresses the opportunities now opened up for the widespread employment of the poor themselves in programmes for the poor, and vigorously advocates, on several grounds, the use of "the indigenous non-professional" in staffing preventive social programmes in all problem areas.*[22]

NON-INSTITUTIONAL METHODS: PROBATION

Clearly a great deal of what has already been said, in connection with institutional treatment, about individualization, typologies, group processes and so on has relevance for non-institutional methods such as probation. In this field a great deal has already been achieved in modifying classical case-work principles and techniques in terms of the social context of court work. The supposed incompatibility between helping and authority functions, for example, has been largely resolved in terms of such concepts as "agency function".[27] Probation officers have never worked exclusively on a one-to-one relationship with their clients and milieu management has, at least in a general sense, always been part of their practice. Group counselling techniques for probationers or their families are increasingly being explored[28] and this could well lead to the establishment of an even wider, supportive, social context for probation work. Perhaps it will eventually be possible to construct some meaningful counterpart or analogue of the institutional therapeutic community in the outside community itself. Who can tell what new roles will then emerge for probation officers, probationers, ex-probationers and all sorts of other people who have remained up till now uninvolved in such work?

* These latter developments are not cited as models to be applied directly to the solution of problems of crime prevention in this country but simply to illustrate additional aspects of the strategy of "involvement".

PREVENTION

In concluding one can only ask what applications does all this have for prevention. In looking at the present situation, it is only too easy to be overwhelmed by a general impression of confusion. At the primary level of broad social services and measures one is confronted by considerable conflict of opinion on how such services should be organized. At the secondary level of measures aimed at vulnerable individuals or groups, one encounters a bewildering range of different schemes and projects and an almost complete lack of co-ordination and communication.

One theme underlying our discussion of penal treatment was that of "integration"—between theory and research and practice, between the institution and the community, between staff and inmates, between types of staff. It is easy to raise similar problems in the field of prevention and much harder to suggest solutions.

Here again, we shall, perhaps, achieve some clarification if we concentrate more on how extensively we should define the patient, the problem, the agent or agency, the objectives and the processes of prevention. Pathology may be seen as located in the total social system, in particular classes or sections of society, at the community level, in various reference or peer-groups, in the family or in the individual. The problem may be defined in more or less abstract terms —as racial deprivation and underprivilege in the widest sense, community disorganization, family breakdown, deviant social behaviour or specific delinquent acts by groups or individuals. The techniques of prevention may be arranged in corresponding fashion. Clearly these alternatives are not mutually exclusive.

Here one can only state the central problem in general terms as that of getting the balance of levels right in devising a properly balanced and co-ordinated set of preventive strategies and suggest that, as in the treatment field, there remains a constant danger of focusing too narrowly on one aspect of the situation at the expense of the rest.

It has recently been pointed out that the trend within the United States is now for preventive policies and schemes to move further away from criminal activity itself and address themselves to conditions "further in back" of delinquency. This, it is suggested, has involved a fusion between sub-cultural approaches and broad policies for changing the social system.[29] The current emphasis on "opportunity theory" would seem to be leading to a more radical attack on the broad fronts of poverty and privilege in order to get at the source of delinquency generally and its sub-cultural forms in particular. A not dissimilar trend can be detected in this country although this tends to be obscured by the current debate on the family as the target of choice for preventive work.

Even so, there is a strong body of opinion that we should go beyond this level of operation and set up an integrated social service on a much more comprehensive scale. Such a service would be justified "in its own right" and not simply for its potential contribution to the reduction of crime and delinquency. This approach would appear to make sense provided it forms part of a properly coordinated strategy of primary prevention which also includes the development of mental health services, educational facilities, employment and leisure opportunities and so on.

One point, however, seems worth making. Measures which merely reinforce the *traditional* roles of the family or the school, for example, will prove to be inadequate and even unhelpful. In a society undergoing rapid social change the realistic aim will have to be that of preparing these social institutions and supporting them in such a way that they will be able to discharge their future social functions in new ways which cannot even be clearly foreseen at any particular point in time.

The improvement of strategies of primary prevention may reduce but will never eliminate the need for a wide diversity of services, schemes and projects beamed at vulnerable groups and individuals. For both theoretical and practical reasons, these methods of secondary prevention may also become more effective if they are applied to more heterogeneous groups whose "vulnerability" is defined in broader terms than "delinquency proneness". It would be naïve to look for some dramatic imaginative break-through in techniques; the realistic aim is to encourage a more vigorous application of the kinds of approach already in use.

One dogmatic assertion is offered in conclusion. At whatever level of prevention we may choose to operate, the key *practical* problem is that of achieving the maximum active involvement not only of those individuals and groups which are "at risk" but of the whole community itself in the widest possible ways. In the last analysis, crime is not simply a threat to society; it is a problem for which society together with the individual must share responsibility.

NOTES AND REFERENCES

1. Fox, Sir Lionel, On the application of penological science, *Br. J. Delinq.* **5** (2), 1954.
2. Gill, H. B., Correctional philosophy and architecture, *J. Crim. Law, Crim. and Pol. Sc.* **53** (3), 1962.
3. See Gibbons, D. C., *Changing the Lawbreaker*, New Jersey, Prentice-Hall, 1965, for an excellent discussion of the relevance of these studies for institutional treatment (pp. 196–220). The footnotes on pp. 194–8 and 212 provide an up-to-date bibliography.
4. McCorkle, Ll. W., and Korn, R., Resocialization within walls, *Ann. Amer. Acad. Polit. Social Sci.* **293**, 1954.
5. Conrad, J. P., *Crime and Its Correction*, London, Tavistock, 1965.
6. See Gibbons, *op. cit.*, note 3.
7. Grant, M. Q., Interaction between kinds of treatments and kinds of delinquents, in Monograph No. 2, California Board of Corrections, 1961.
8. Sutherland, E. H., The person and the situation in the treatment of prisoners, in Cohen, A., Lindesmith, A., and Scheussler (Ed.), *The Sutherland Papers*, Indiana University Press, 1956.
9. Polsky, N., *Cottage Six*, Russell Sage Foundation, 1962.
10. Goldsmith, J. M., Schulman, R., and Grossbard, H., Integrating clinical processes with planned living experiences, *Amer. J. Orthopsychiat.* **24** (2), 1954.
11. The most comprehensive theoretical analysis of community therapy is that of Rapaport, R. N., *Community as Doctor*, London, Tavistock, 1960. For an introduction to the subject see: Clark, D. H., The therapeutic community—concept, practice and future, *Br. J. Psychiat.* **111**, No. 479, 1965; and Taylor, F. H., The treatment of delinquent psychopaths, *Howard J.* **11** (2), 1963. For further reading see Jones, M., *Social Psychiatry in the Community, in Hospitals and in Prisons*, Illinois, Thomas, 1962; The treatment of character disorders, *Br. J. Crim.* **3** (3), 1963; and What has psychiatry to learn from penology? *Br. J. Crim.* **4** (3), 1964.
12. Wilson, J. M., The role of the therapeutic community in correctional institutions of the future, in *The Future of Imprisonment in a Free Society*, Chicago, St. Leonard's House, 1965.
13. Tollinton, H. P., The psychological treatment of abnormal offenders, *Prison Service J.* **5** (20), 1966.
14. Miller, D., *Growth to Freedom*, London, Tavistock, 1964.
15. For a discussion of the early counselling developments in this country, see Morrison, R. L., Group counselling in penal institutions, *Howard J.* **10** (2), 1961. For a more general account, see *New Psychological Methods for the Treatment of Prisoners* (and preparatory papers by Fenton, N., Colin, M., de Berker, P., Sturup, G. K., Larsson, S., and Elias, A.), Brussels International Penal and Penitentiary Foundation, 1962.
16. Conrad, *op. cit.*, note 5, pp. 236–48.
17. de Berker, P., The sociology of change in penal institutions, in Klare, H. J. (Ed.), *Changing Concepts of Crime and Its Treatment*, Oxford, Pergamon Press, 1966.
18. For examples of the changing roles of specialists working in the approved school field, see Connell, P. H., A psychiatrist joins the staff of an approved school, *Br. J. Crim.* **5** (1), 1965; and Views on psychiatry and approved schools (bibliography), *Br. J. Crim.* **5** (2), 1965.

19. KASSEBAUM, G. G., WARD, D. A., and WILNER, D. M., Group treatment by correctional personnel, Monograph no. 3, California Board of Corrections, 1963.

20. CRESSEY, D. R., Theoretical foundations for using criminals in the rehabilitation of criminals, in *The Future of Imprisonment in a Free Society*, Chicago, St. Leonard's House, 1965. A revised version of the above appears in the *J. Res. in Crime and Delinq.* **2**, (2), 1965, under the title of Social psychological foundations for using criminals in the rehabilitation of criminals.

21. Synanon is a voluntary organization which provides a specialized form of group and community therapy for drug addicts in an open residential setting. For a general descriptive account of these methods see YABLONSKY, L., *The Tunnel Back*, New York, Macmillan, 1965; and CASRIEL, D., *So Fair a House*, New York, Prentice-Hall, 1963.

22. PEARL, A., and REISSMAN, F., *New Careers for the Poor*, New York, The Free Press, 1965.

23. *Experiment in Culture Expansion*, National Institute of Mental Health, U.S. Department of Health, Education and Welfare, 1963.

24. *A Proposal for the Prevention and Control of Delinquency by Expanding Opportunities*, 2nd ed., New York, Mobilization for Youth, Inc., 1962.

25. *Youth in the Ghetto*, New York, Haryou, 1964.

26. OHLIN, LL. E., and CLOWARD, R., *Delinquency and Opportunity*, London, Routledge and Kegan Paul, 1961.

27. MORRISON, R. L., Authority and treatment, in *The Concept of Authority*, Shotton Hall, 1966. See especially pp. 6–8 and References.

28. Several short articles on this topic will be found in *Probation*, **11**(3), 1965, and **12** (1), 1966. Various articles describing American practice appear in *Crime and Delinq.* **11** (4), 1965.

29. LEJINS, P. P., Recent changes in the concept of prevention, in *Proc. Amer. Correctional Assoc.* 1965.

VI

PREVENTION AND TREATMENT

10. PREVENTION

As Mr. R. L. Morrison (XX) indicates, the prevention of crime is not one subject but many. The preventive measures can operate at different levels of society, and prevention can be directed at persons of different degrees of criminal sophistication, or at those who are merely potentially delinquent. Furthermore, one aspect of prevention not touched upon by Mr. Morrison must concern the opportunities presented to those who are "at risk". Current public attitudes towards crime are potent factors in determining the readiness of the potential criminal to attempt certain crimes, and such attitudes may also be reflected in the readiness of members of the public to help the police.

The relationship between police and public is considered by Mr. B. N. Bebbington (III). It is perhaps interesting to recall that the Congress was held only a few days after the murder of three policemen in London, which caused a great wave of public sympathy for the police. Mr. Bebbington comments on the difficulty of assessing public feeling and on the apparent fluctuations in attitude. "Sympathy for the police seems to alternate pretty regularly with antipathy." The Royal Commission on the Police (1962) tried to establish the facts about public attitudes by means of a survey: this showed that 80 per cent of those interviewed strongly supported the police.

The element of partnership between police and public in the policing of the country is of great importance. Yet "few people know even what the Common Law of this country demands of them in the way of police duties". It should be clear that if such a partnership is to be effective and have any meaning, the public must know what is expected of it. And yet knowledge itself is unlikely to affect the readiness of the public to become closely involved in law enforcement. Current attitudes towards the law and police will largely determine this.

In the increasingly complex society in which we now live, with its multitude of administrative regulations, the boundaries between right and wrong, honesty and dishonesty, have perhaps become blurred. Even the most scrupulous man will one day find himself a traffic offender; and the opportunities for scrounging or fiddling, with no moral stigma, are legion. It is perhaps harder to identify with the forces of law enforcement when you are conscious of your own lapses into illegality, and the experience of being an offender, common now to motorists, often strengthens unhelpful attitudes towards the police.

In an attempt to improve contact between the police and public in urban areas, the traditional type of policing by constables on the beat is being superseded in some towns by experimental methods. In these, a constable becomes, as it were, a resident unit, living on or near his beat. There is also a 24 hour cover by a police officer in a motor-car. It is hoped that urban dwellers will once again be encouraged by having their own local policeman, and that relations with the public will improve as a result.

Crime prevention by the police is of a specific kind. But there is also general prevention. This can be defined as action aimed specifically at reducing the criminogenic factors in society as a whole, or in defined communities. It would, for example, be concerned with the social and cultural problems of high delinquency areas. At present individuals from high delinquency areas who become offenders are still dealt with as cases of individual breakdown—by probation officers, or child guidance clinics, or police liaison officers, or children's departments. In fact, the greater part of the resources of the personal social services are probably deployed in such areas, and yet very little attempt is made to tackle the social and cultural problems of the areas in which individual problem cases occur with such frequency.

The phenomenon of the high delinquency area has been well investigated and described, both in this country (e.g. by T. Morris and J. B. Mays) and elsewhere (e.g. in the Chicago studies of Shaw and Mackay). Very little has been done, however, to develop methods for effecting community change. Attempts to improve "bad" areas have generally been concerned with the physical environment and the provision of facilities (e.g. youth clubs or clinics), but the problems presented by community attitudes which are at variance with those of the wider community have only been tackled at the level of individual cases.

We must now give thought to the techniques of community development, and at the same time consider concepts of community health which are concerned not merely with the community's inclination to crime and deviant moral standards, but with the total functioning of the community and its effects upon the well-being of the individuals who compose it. Such concepts must recognize the wide variety of cultural patterns which are valid within the framework of our society, and must not seek to prove the moral superiority of middle-class values. We must develop methods for utilizing the strengths of a community in order to overcome its *malaise* (*Stress and Release in an Urban Community*, Spencer *et al.*)

In the school, the problems of the community and of the individual can be seen to merge. Schools provide a possible means of observing the potential delinquent and bringing to bear upon him various services designed to forestall his lapse into delinquency. In addition, however, the school provides a small community which will to some extent be able to influence its own delinquency level by the quality of its own community life, and in so far as a school is successful in containing the delinquent tendencies of its pupils, it can be seen as an institution capable of exercising an important influence on the larger community to which it belongs and from which its pupils are drawn.

In his paper on this subject, Mr. J. McNally (XVIII) emphasizes that schools are still struggling to find the means for dealing with their *educational* deviants. The Newsom Report has indicated the failure of the schools to cater satisfactorily for the children of lower intelligence. The diagnosis of the maladjusted and the educationally subnormal is still gravely inadequate, and suitable education for these children is often lacking. Child guidance clinics have long waiting lists on which there are quite a number of children who should not be going to a psychiatrist but need other forms of help.

There have been recent developments in remedial education, and some improvement in the school psychological services. A government committee is currently inquiring into the need for educational psychologists. Nevertheless, amongst these children who are undiagnosed or unprovided for, there are many who are, or will become, delinquent. But faced with the problems of their educational deviants, schools have no common urge to do anything about the problems of delinquency. Delinquency is of varied incidence, and some schools have little experience of it, so that teachers generally do not view it as a broad general problem.

There is a lack of basic information about delinquency at local level. What is a high delinquency rate in an area? Which schools have an unduly high proportion of delinquents and which have a surprisingly low proportion, bearing in mind the social environment? How do current figures compare with previous years in this or that neighbourhood, street or school? Important questions such as these can only be answered against a background of local statistics, kept from year to year. But at present local record-keeping is fragmentary, and no one has the responsibility of maintaining all the essential information.

There is, however, a growing movement amongst educationists that the schools must play a bigger part in the diagnosis, prevention and treatment of delinquency. It can no longer be considered merely a "fringe" topic. The current controversy on comprehensive schools, together with such studies as Douglas's *Home and School*, are re-emphasizing the importance of environmental factors in education, and are perhaps already modifying the criticism that education departments are less alive than they should be to the social problems of children in normal schools.

There is some evidence to show that schools can have a direct influence on the level of delinquency. As the result of an inquiry in the West Riding of Yorkshire, Sir Alec Clegg found that the delinquency rates of various schools showed no correlation with the assessed social qualities of the surrounding neighbourhood, but a positive correlation existed between delinquency rates and certain schools. This work was not undertaken to research standards, but is confirmed by studies now being undertaken in London. Gross and consistent differences are found in the delinquency rates of a number of secondary schools, with no relationship apparent between the schools' rates and the social qualities of their neighbourhoods.

The recipe for the success of the "good" school in the "bad" area is not known, and awaits detailed socio-psychological investigation. Useful results may come from a continuation of Power and Phillipson's work in London, from Rose in the Central Lancashire Family and Community Project, or from the Constructive Education Project organized by the National Foundation for Educational Research. Hidden delinquency which goes unrecorded sets a problem by throwing doubt on the validity of such data as are available; and research cannot be expected to produce easy answers for teachers who want to know how to treat delinquents.

The schools may play a part in the preventive measures of the larger community by helping to educate the community. But schools must also recognize that it is beyond their capacity to offer effective help to children with personality disorders or suffering from acute emotional disturbance.

Whilst some schools have helped to counter delinquency, others, by their failure to recognize the personal problems of some children, have actively promoted delinquents. Recognition of the potentially delinquent or potentially disturbed child at a stage when his delinquent or disturbed behaviour has not become manifest is an extremely difficult problem, yet necessary if successful preventive treatment is to be applied. There has been much work done on the prediction of delinquents in America; and in this country Stott's Bristol Social Adjustment Guide provides an easy means for screening children and isolating those who need treatment.

The schools could make their best contribution to prevention by making education more meaningful and attainable for children of diverse temperaments and all levels of ability. The work of Reckless has shown that a child's self-concept is the most certain insulator against delinquency. A major task for all schools is to ensure that academic achievement is not the sole measure of what is worth while. Schools in poor social areas must aim to affect the aspirations and attitudes of the community, and towards this purpose much can be learned from some of the current American demonstration projects in (or linked with) schools.

In his keynote lecture, Mr. R. L. Morrison (XX) refers to the trend in the United States "for preventive policies and schemes to move further away from criminal activity itself and address themselves to conditions 'further in back' of delinquency". The same concern to see preventive policies in a wider and yet more fundamental sense is apparent in Miss Joan Cooper's (IX) paper on "Local Authorities and Preventive Work".

Historically, the prevention of crime and juvenile delinquency has not been an important commitment for local authorities. According to Caplan's concepts of primary, secondary and tertiary prevention, primary prevention is a community concept and entails making readily avilable to all sections of the community advice and help for those faced with high risk situations, such as bereavement, illness, injury or marital difficulties. Secondary preventive programmes aim at early diagnosis and effective treatment with a view to avoiding chronic anti-social conduct or permanent maladjustment or illness. Tertiary preventive programmes aim at rehabilitation.

Within the local authorities, services have been developed to meet particular needs, and have only been concerned with delinquency as an off-shoot of their main purpose. The schools and youth service have provided a primary preventive service, but schools are not basically therapeutic institutions and so secondary preventive functions have been developed by child guidance clinics and the school psychological service.

The need to co-ordinate local authority services in order to provide effective preventive measures has been recognized for many years. In 1949 a joint circular was issued by the Home Office and the Ministry of Education on the prevention of juvenile delinquency; and in 1950 these two ministries, together with the Ministry of Health, issued a circular on *Children Neglected or Ill-treated in their own Homes*. Both circulars emphasized the need for early preventive action to avoid deprivation and delinquency.

From the second circular came suggestions for co-ordination, although the arrangements made for bringing together the personnel of different departments have not always been successful, and were, indeed, criticized by the Ingleby Committee (Cmnd. 1191, 1960.) Nevertheless, there has been much joint effort, particularly towards solving the problems of multi-problem families, and in some areas efforts have been made to provide imaginative treatment for both mothers and children from such families.

Local authorities seem generally reluctant to undertake a primary preventive function beyond that already provided by schools and the health visitor service. Social services are regarded as residual services for breakdown, and the authorities are slow to undertake a wider function. The 1963 Children and Young Persons Act gave clear primary functions to children's departments, yet family advice centres have not been developed to any great extent to make available the services of the local authority to those at risk and in need of support.

Changes in our society have decreased the ability of the family, including the normally competent family, to meet crises from its own resources. In 1963, 25,000 children were received into the care of local authorities because of the short-term illness or confinement of the mother. Because services have been developed to meet certain needs, there has been a tendency for each service to view people from the point of view of its own agency function.

But today we need services which are not only available to all, but also comprehensive, so that assessment, information, advice, referral to the appropriate worker, and treatment, all reflect not only the perspectives of the specialist services, but also a comprehensive view of the individual, his family and his neighbourhood. "It is arguable that only when there is an integrated diagnostic and treatment service available will local authorities be enabled to play a major part in crime prevention. It is also arguable that this stage will only be reached when all the local services are promotional as well as crisis intervention services". Such matters are under review by the Seebohm Committee at the present time, and the report of that committee may well be available by the time these Proceedings are published.

Local authorities may have tended to view delinquency only as a symptom, or a particular variety of disturbed behaviour, and so have not made special provision for delinquents. Dr. Peter Scott has urged an opposite view, that delinquents show definite differences from maladjusted or deprived children. And yet in the end, delinquency is a socially defined administrative category. It therefore remains to be argued whether delinquent behaviour should be treated so far as possible within the community, by services designed to provide diagnosis and treatment for many types of disturbed behaviour, or whether special provision should be made for delinquents. Are there perhaps dangers in categorizing children too closely? Too little is known as yet of the possible effect on a child of identifying him as a member of a delinquent group, but Grygier has suggested that this may in itself have harmful effects.

There is now a large measure of agreement that much disturbed behaviour amongst adults, whether in the form of mental illness, criminal behaviour, or inadequacy in parental or other functions, has roots in childhood deprivation. Effective preventive measures must therefore be taken in the pre-school years. In the field of physical health, great advances have been made through health visitors and environmental health services. It is now time to tackle problems of emotional, social and cultural deprivation. Dr. Kellmer Pringle has stressed the need for early intervention to prevent the problems which can arise from cultural deprivation and limited speech development. Bernstein and Safir show the effect of language on the development of cultural divisions, and a greater use of nursery schools could perhaps go some way to combat the effects of cultural deprivation.

Meanwhile, progress is being made. Children's departments are becoming increasingly aware of the scope offered by their newly acquired functions of primary prevention. A considerable number of departments are now claiming to be dealing with more children in their own homes than are in the care of the local authority. Moreover, case-work services are increasingly working with, and through, the family and neighbourhood of the deviant individual. The next step might appear to be a more consciously planned preventive strategy. We have learned that it is not sufficient to provide social services without also offering social workers who can help those in need to accept the service. Perhaps we are now moving towards an extension of the concept of accountability into this field of local authority preventive work, so that the service becomes accountable for those who need help but do not voluntarily use the service.

At certain times people are subject to particular stresses which may render them peculiarly liable to some form of social breakdown. If such times can be identified, they may provide points of focus for preventive services. The period of transition from school to work coincides with an age group which has a high level of delinquency and it has been thought that the difficulties faced by young people at this time may have some relevance to delinquency-proneness. This was in fact one of the subjects being investigated by the short-lived Advisory Committee on Juvenile Delinquency which was set up by the Home Secretary in 1964.

In considering the problems of this period of transition, Dr. M. E. M. Herford (XIV) asserts that school-leaving occurs at a time which is critical for many young people; a phase of metamorphosis which involves processes of self-realization and identification. It is difficult for schools to meet the needs of young people at this stage. In addition, the varying ages at which young people achieve bio-logical maturity cannot be accommodated to administrative con-venience—and we are planning to raise the school-leaving age still further whilst being told that young people are maturing earlier. In these circumstances, school for some of these young people becomes detention in the name of education; and whilst calling it a privilege we make it compulsory. Inevitably, some rebel.

The actual transition from school to work may be a traumatic ex-perience, and there is no adequate provision for phasing it out. When they start work, young people are able to earn money easily, but have few responsibilities. In addition, they are subject to the considerable pressures of mass media and advertising. Young people who are unsure of their identity, and who have not matured through responsiblity, are extremely vulnerable to such pressures. At this time they need support and help in establishing for themselves good standards and attitudes. On leaving school, the better or more conformist boys will probably be selected by better firms, and are more likely to get good handling and support through training schemes or apprenticeships. Those even more fortunate may go on to college or university, where they are helped by a tutorial system and a good student health service. For the socially underprivileged and the handicapped, either physically or mentally, there is no one with a responsibility.

Various services impinge on this problem—the youth service, the youth employment service, the probation service, etc. There is an obvious need for greater co-operation between them. The Appointed Factory Doctor is also provided with a special opportunity for early preventive action because his statutory responsibilities give him regular and frequent contact with young people. It is therefore to be regretted that a recent departmental report has recommended, in effect, the abolition of the functions of the Appointed Factory Doctor.

The objectives of prevention can be seen narrowly in terms of crime and delinquency or in more extensive terms. Similarly, as Mr. Morrison (XX) points out: "Pathology may be seen as located in the total social system, in particular classes or sections of society, at the community level, in various reference or peer-groups, or in the family or in the individual". The techniques of prevention are as varied as the definition of the problem, and alternative techniques are not mutually exclusive. The urgent need, however, is for some agreement on priorities, and properly planned and co-ordinated strategies of preventive action, both at national and local level.

11. THE COMMUNITY AND ITS REJECTS

There are certain people within our society who pose problems not so much because their behaviour presents a real threat or danger to others in any material or physical sense, but because they deviate from the standards generally accepted by the community.

Dr. H. M. Holden (XV) in his paper "Adolescence and Delinquency", surveys the attitude of the community from the point of view of a psycho-analyst.

Recently, the word "teenager" has become almost synonymous with the word "delinquent" in the public mind. There is a public image of adolescence, with its sensational overtones of violence, delinquency and promiscuity. Whilst acknowledging that there has been, in recent years, a real and disturbing increase in adolescent crime, it is questionable whether this, in itself, justifies the public image. Is it possible that the public image itself may be a contributory factor to the increase in delinquency?

Over the past 10 years there has been a steadily widening split between the adult and adolescent sections of the community. Adolescence has always been a time of rebellion and adolescents have always constituted a threat to "their elders and betters" although in the past the adults have been able to cope with this threat. When any deviant group arises in a society it creates an internal threat to the remainder which is based partly on envy. Adolescents are envied for their spontaneity, their freedom, their ability to discard outworn modes of thinking and behaviour, their freshness and their attractiveness; and society finds profoundly disquieting such details as their mode of dress and their hair styles.

This threat and the envy that is behind it is often dealt with by the mechanism of projection or scapegoating. This is a traditional method of dealing with deviants. The Jews, for example, have been persistently persecuted for over 2000 years because of their determination to remain "different", and such details as the shape of a nose, the wearing of hats and worshipping on Saturday rather than Sunday assume a symbolic significance which constitutes a great threat to the remainder. The Jews have become scapegoats for the projected faults of the community.

It may be that adolescents are now the scapegoats of modern Western society and that their rebellion and deviation from accepted norms are far more threatening than in former times. The public image of the "teenager" is the pillory into which they have been placed by the community. The reasons for this new threat are, firstly, adolescent affluence (an entirely new phenomenon); secondly, the mass communication media; thirdly, exploitation by certain sections of commerce, notably the press, television, recording and clothing industries. These sections have cashed in on adolescent rebellion and affluence by the creation of a synthetic "pop" teenage culture. As a result, teenagers are seen as especially menacing on account of their increased wealth and power. The "pop" image stresses all the sensational and decadent aspects of adolescence, and adolescents themselves feel forced into accepting this role, or at least dressing the part.

Even though some resent this situation and rebel against it, this very rebellion can itself be exploited. Thus the "beatnik" movement, originally a spontaneous rebellion against commercialization, has now been the object of a take-over bid by the recording industry, with the creation of synthetic millionaire professional beatniks.

The successors to the beatniks are the "unattached", the homeless, rootless youngsters who drift in increasing numbers into the large cities and soon become caught up in the criminal underworld. The most serious aspect of their problem is that they have given up rebelling and live only for "kicks" through drugs or sex or crime. These are society's rejects, and although they are the community's responsibility, as yet nothing has been done by society to help them, perhaps because of its need to maintain them in a scapegoat role.

Immigrants inevitably cause concern in any community because they bring with them a different cultural background, their own particular way of doing things, their own values and beliefs. Immigrant groups often become the objects of hostility because their behaviour is unacceptable. But what evidence is there that immigrants to this country make any special contribution to the pattern or volume of crime?

Mr. A. E. Bottoms (V), in a paper on "Delinquency Among Immigrants", notes that no specific empirical research has yet been carried out, although some is just beginning at the Institute of Race Relations. There have been a number of books written on social aspects of immigration into Britain, but the writers have barely touched upon the subject of crime. British criminologists, and notably F. H. McClintock, have provided some data in the course of researches directed primarily to other ends, but no very firm conclusions can be drawn. This is because where such data seem to show differential crime rates for certain groups, the interpretation of the correlations is not possible without more information about the social and economic situations of the groups.

It is possible to say that crime rates for Irish immigrants seem to be generally high, even when like age is compared to like, but that this pattern has apparently remained steady for several years. Commonwealth immigrants, on the other hand, tend to have relatively low crime rates except in relation to crimes of violence. However, a close study of McClintock's work reveals the importance of domestic disputes among Commonwealth immigrants, so that, for example, if domestic disputes are excluded from the analysis, the proportion of Commonwealth immigrants among all violent offenders in London actually fell between 1957 and 1960. Moreover, studies undertaken in Bradford and Bedfordshire show that Commonwealth immigrants tend not to commit offences against property, such as breaking and entering, or larceny. One can safely conclude that there is not a general "immigrant crime problem" in this country—that at least relative to other criminal problems, crime among immigrants is not a major social problem.

Nevertheless, "the relation of immigration to crime . . . is a problem of first-rate importance from the point of view of a theory of criminality and of legislative and administrative policies" (Sutherland and Cressey). One reform that is necessary from both these points of view is the inclusion of the country of origin among the social data in the criminal statistics. Objections to this are, it is submitted, ill-founded.

But even if this is done, further research is needed to test the formulations about immigrant crime derived from research in the United States and in Israel. Clearly, just as crime rates may vary among immigrant groups from different countries of origin, so they may vary amongst immigrants from any one country going to host societies with different social conditions. Among American results it would be helpful to test in Britain are the findings that immigrant crime rates tend to be higher in communities which do not keep themselves together in "colonies" or tightly knit groups in a city, and that the second generation have a higher crime rate than the first generation. In relation to the second generation of Commonwealth immigrants in this country such research could be linked with programmes of social action and delinquency prevention.

To present one possible hypothesis which might be tested, it may be that if a second generation could be more closely integrated with the native community through the school playing a socially creative role in various ways, this might meet the desire for assimilation by the young immigrants and reduce the need to be delinquent as a rebellion against failure to achieve adequate integration. (Such a programme accords with what J. McNally (XVIII) has to say on the role of the school in the prevention and treatment of delinquency: *see* p.107).

General theoretical formulations about immigration, already fairly plentiful, also need to be tested by research. Not one has so far emerged that is fully convincing, and it is probable that advances in theory in this area must await the collection of more information—particularly information relating to the detail of immigrant crime patterns—so that we cease talking about "crime rates" in blanket fashion. For example, a good theory needs to explain why, in Britain, Irish immigrants have in general a high robbery rate—but hardly ever rob from private premises or after previous association; and why housebreaking is conspicuously absent among the crimes of Commonwealth immigrants.

Furthermore, theory needs to take more account than hitherto of the type of person who becomes an immigrant, since immigrants obviously do not represent a random sample of their native populations. For example, a study by Ødegaard of Norwegians in Minnesota showed that Norwegians with a schizoid character were more likely to emigrate than others, so that post-migratory mental disorders were not simply a failure to adjust to the new society.

Immigrant offenders present certain special difficulties in sentencing and treatment. They are now subject to deportation, but very little is known about the operation of this sentence or its deterrent effect. Sentencers sometimes need to exercise especial care in view of the sensitivity of public opinion about immigrant crime. Those involved in treatment face difficulties of cross-cultural communication, and there is some evidence that these are best surmounted by taking a group of immigrants together for treatment.

In passing, Mr. Bottoms notes that one offence which Commonwealth immigrants commit more frequently than others is being in possession of dangerous drugs. In his paper on drug-taking, Mr. Arthur Chisnall (VI) does not consider any of the statistical information available, but puts forward some controversial ideas about the causes of the recent increase in drug-taking amongst young people. He suggests that drug-taking is essentially a reaction to society's failure to provide creative outlets for leisure. It follows on this view that in the right social setting, accompanied by continuing social support, young people will have little inclination to take drugs. Mr. Chisnall's own Jazz Club project on Eel Pie Island is quoted in support of this view.

Drug-taking and its effects are both seen to a large extent as culturally determined phenomena. In different sub-cultural groups there are certain drugs which are favoured at any particular time. Different cultures also have their own modes of addictive behaviour, and addiction to drugs must therefore be seen as significant in reflecting a certain type of society. Addiction is seen as protest behaviour, the object of addiction being chosen because it is offensive to the establishment. Where protest is the result of feeling not merely opposed but actually defeated by society, the permanent solution to the addictive behaviour lies in restoring hope and confidence. The non-conformists must also be given special attention, as they may be the innovators of tomorrow.

In his paper on "Sex Deviance and Community Attitudes", Mr. Michael Schofield (XXV) begins by reminding us that deviance is a word with meaning only in the context of a particular society. Deviant behaviour is only recognized as such because it deviates from a conformity imposed by the community. It is often thought of as a legal problem, and sometimes as a medical problem. In fact, it is also a sociological problem, since deviant behaviour is deviance not from a universal, natural law, but from the norm of a particular society.

As an example of this, one can consider how adultery and pre-marital intercourse are now largely accepted and evoke only slight disapproval, whereas at one time they would have been clearly seen as deviant behaviour. Homosexuality is now the best documented and most widespread form of deviant behaviour. It is also a matter of concern to the criminal law. Lesbianism appears to be more easily accepted and has not been the subject of much special research.

Community attitudes to homosexuality have changed considerably in the last 20 years. Even after the publication of the Wolfenden Report in 1957 there was a majority of the public opposed to changing the law; but a national survey conducted in 1965 for a religious television programme showed that only 25 per cent of those interviewed thought homosexual offences should be punished, whilst 27 per cent condemned but did not wish for punishment, and 36 per cent thought they should be tolerated.

There is also other evidence of a community shift towards more tolerant attitudes. The reaction of any individual to homosexual activities depends upon his age, his religion and his own personality. Those who have to resist homosexual temptations themselves are often those who are most vehement against changing the law. Those who have met several homosexuals tend to be more tolerant than those who have not met any.

This shift towards greater tolerance shows in two ways. One attitude is to think of homosexual men as being sick and in need of psychiatric treatment. The other is to view social deviance in the light of its social harm.

If homosexuality is a pathological condition, then it must be one of the most common psychological disorders known. If it is a medical problem, then it is clear that treatment has so far been remarkably unsuccessful.

There is a growing tendency to view all forms of sexual deviance as conditions requiring a medical solution. Those who have experience of marital or personal problems, however, are generally agreed that sexual "deviance" is far more common than is apparent or generally admitted. In fact, deviant behaviour of one kind or another is part of the particular social organization we have evolved. It is part of the social cost. Getting rid of it may only be possible if we are prepared to undertake a fundamental reorganization of our social structure, and this we are not likely to be willing to embark upon. Consequently, we should regard sexual deviances, like all forms of deviant behaviour, in the light of their social harm. Some forms of deviance may arouse strong emotions, but the law should only be invoked to deal with deviance which is socially harmful.

12. CLASSIFICATION

In his keynote lecture, Mr. R. L. Morrison (XX) discusses the problem of individualization of treatment. He notes (p. 86) that "simply to insist on the uniqueness or idiosyncrasy of the individual case prevents the development of any rational system of diagnosis and treatment since this inevitably depends on some process of classifying and generalizing".

Indeed, one interpretation of individualization is to see this as allocating the offender to a treatment programme which most approximates to his needs, rather than envisaging a specially prepared programme for each offender. The process of classifying the offender goes on at various stages in the progress from arrest to treatment, and on to discharge, and at each stage the options are different. A person on arrest can be released on bail, or detained in custody, and although this is in itself not a decision about treatment, it is nevertheless a classification and a decision which may have repercussions on treatment. The court has to make difficult sentencing decisions which include a choice between institutional treatment or treatment in the open. Within the framework of the institutional system there is further classification to allocate the offender to the most appropriate of the available institutions. Within the institution there are groups receiving different types of training and treatment. And, finally, the situation is now being reached where the availability of certain kinds of after-care provision depends on the offender being classified in a certain way.

In his paper on "New Issues and Techniques in Sentencing", Mr. J. E. Hall Williams (XXX) draws on some of his experiences in the United States. In Britain, the trial judge fixes not only the nature of the sentence but, in the case of imprisonment, the length of the term (subject to the rules governing remission). The proposals for a parole system, under which prisoners will be eligible for release after serving only one-third of their sentence, introduce interesting questions about how we know when a person is ready for release and who should decide this. In the United States the indeterminate sentence is widely used. In the case of a prison sentence the judge may have no dis-cretion about the length of sentence. The law fixes the term, usually with a minimum and a maximum, and the decision about the date of release is taken by the prison administration within the prescribed limits, with or without the help of a parole board. Alternatively, the judge may fix the minimum and maximum term within the limits the law lays down, and the effect will be much the same in that someone other than the trial judge will decide when the offender is ready to be released.

Two minor issues present themselves at this point. Firstly, do our maximum sentences reflect the values of modern society? Secondly, should the minimum term be fixed by the judge or by the law? Ex-perience in the United States is that both judge-fixed and statutory minima constantly stand in the way of enlightened penal admini-stration.

The major issue is whether judges should sentence at all, and whether the penal system would be improved by a system of in-determinate sentences. Mr. Hall Williams admits that his visit to the United States has convinced him of some of the merits of an in-determinate system, whilst its drawbacks seem less significant. American opinion itself is divided on the matter, and in practice the really important questions are less about the form of sentence than about the manner in which the release dates are decided and the nature of the prison system itself. We already have indeterminacy in the borstal system and in the case of life sentences and there might be some advantage in experimenting with additional categories of offender.

The United States is usually regarded as having particularly long sentences for certain categories of offence, such as rape, armed robbery and kidnapping. Recent events in Britain have shown that we may well be about to follow in the same direction, and there is much anxiety about the meaning of all this and its possible effects on the penal system. The American reputation may be undeserved for, in California at least, the ordinary housebreaker or burglar serves no longer than he would here. Moreover, there is a considerable awareness of the need to study violence and the dangerous offender, as demonstrated by several programmes in California such as the Stress Assessment Unit. In a scientific age we cannot afford to ignore opportunities to study violent and dangerous individuals. Better research and more adequate preventive measures may save lives. There is no case for a return to methods, such as capital punishment, which have little or no relevance to the problem.

In the United States the idea of judicial review of sentencing decisions by an appeal court has hardly been recognized and there is nothing comparable to the extensive jurisdiction exercised in this country by the Court of Criminal Appeal (now the Criminal Division of the Court of Appeal). There is now a proposal being hotly debated for the federal system to adopt something on these lines. However, federal judges do have a useful opportunity for second thoughts about a sentence. Since 1946 they have had the power to reduce a sentence within 60 days. A provision of this kind might be very helpful in this country.

A proposal under consideration in the United States is for sentences, at least in serious cases, to be deemed tentative for a period of one year. During this time the prison authorities would be permitted to petition the court to re-sentence the offender if it appeared to the administration that the sentence was based on a misapprehension as to the history, character or physical or mental condition of the offender.

In Britain, especially since the Streatfield Report (1961), there has been an increase in the provision of pre-sentence reports, and similar developments have taken place in the United States. Nearly all states have some provision for reports, and at least one, New Jersey, demands a pre-sentence report in all cases. There are no disputes about the need for more information about the offender, but there is some conflict of opinion about the confidentiality of court reports.

The problems of classification within the institutional system are considered by Vernon Holloway (XVI) in his paper "The Future of Classification". Traditionally classification of offenders has been directed towards answering questions such as:

> What degree of control or security does this person need?
> What opportunities can we give him for trade training, psychiatric treatment, educational projects?
> Where are the offenders of similar age, criminal sophistication, intelligence or even personality?

In the administration of the institutional system other questions arise such as the availability of places, or the need to keep certain individuals apart. It becomes difficult in practice to separate classification from what is more properly called administration and management. Moreover, when a number of different regimes are available for the distribution of offenders, the characteristics of each unit which appear important to the classifier may have different significance for the offender. A unit provided for those needing conditions of maximum security may have a reputation for hardness amongst inmates; within one sentence of the court one regime can be known as longer or shorter, harder or softer than another, and so be regarded as more or less punishing. The classification board may be seen as yet another body passing judgement, and so it may become difficult for the Board to maintain the distinctions which seem important to it.

Unlike what happens in many other disciplines classification in criminology has to try to satisfy many needs which often overlap or compete. In modern medicine, for example, one has increasing refinement of the classification of ailments and of treatments for these ailments, and this has been essentially a scientific process. Progress in dealing with offenders has followed a pattern of offering increasing opportunities to many who are not systematically differentiated in terms of predicted response, and this is essentially a humanitarian process.

However, new approaches to classification are now gaining ground. There is a recognition that the differences between regimes can not be assessed merely in terms of levels of security or of the availability or absence of certain facilities. The importance of differences in personal approach in different regimes is slowly being recognized as a matter of significance in the allocation of offenders. Research results, largely coming from California, lead us to hope that, after the results of different kinds of approach with different kinds of offender have been carefully examined, we may be able to state with some degree of objective certainty what the training needs are of any given offender and his chances of responding to an appropriate course. Such assessments may indeed be able to indicate statistically the different chances of successful treatment resulting from different courses of action.

Whilst these two approaches to classification have been contrasted, it is far from certain how far they are actually in opposition to each other. Both have as an ideal the matching of the individual's needs with the available treatment resources. A middle position probably has to be found, because most penal systems will be anxious both to utilize the results of interaction studies such as those in California, and at the same time to preserve a position in which criteria other than those to do with the treatment of the offender can still play a part. Before there can be much progress, however, there must be more explicit statements of the priorities and criteria to be adopted. For example, if it is established that we ought to be treating anxious offenders in one way and the less anxious in another, we must decide whether this new factor will operate instead of or in addition to criteria already in operation for classifying by security risk, degree of criminal sophistication, age, intelligence and so on.

Mr. Holloway surveys a number of points of development in our approach to classification. Much penal classification has been preoccupied with the presence or absence of mental illness; this has largely been because of the question of responsibility and the problem of legal categories affecting the decision of the court. The need of the court to categorize and to establish certain clear-cut distinctions has resulted in a tendency towards similar thinking in penal classification generally. Labels are used as if they indicated definable types when it might be more useful to think in terms of continua along which people are variously distributed; we meet "the psychopath" and "the inadequate offender". The problem of classification is that it is concerned with decreasingly specific entities. One eliminates the psychotic, the subnormal, and one is left with a large residual heterogeneous group. Attempts at differentiation within this group have been of limited value, resulting in the quasi-clinical label without a very specific treatment indication. Examples of such label are "the homosexual", "the withdrawn", "the emotionally disturbed".

As methods of clinical inquiry become more sophisticated, greater precision can be expected based on observed differences. In the meantime we must be vigorous in breaking down categories until specific treatment needs have been isolated, and if specific treatment needs do not emerge we should be ready to question the value of the classification being used. We must also bear in mind that it is possible to make recommendations about a specific section of a population without having to try to provide categories of similar logical order for the rest of that population, thus overstretching a thesis.

There has been a tendency to use for purposes of classification words which are taken over from common usage. Such words have generally not been redefined, so that where the original was vague or ill-defined these features have remained. Many of the words, such as "feckless", "immature", "irresponsible", "inadequate", have a combined descriptive and emotive function which differs from person to person. The words are unsatisfactory even when their emotive content is recognized, because their reliability between one user and another is so low—that is, the same expression may be used by two different people to cover groups or ranges of offenders with only a small degree of overlap.

Perhaps the most significant development in classification is the use of more sophisticated methods derived from research, which attempt to relate groups of offenders to treatment methods. The need to develop treatment-orientated typologies is referred to by Miss Joy Mott (p.22). In the classical PICO study (Pilot Intensive Counselling Organization, California 1955) it was noted that treatment made no appreciable difference to success rates over the total population. However, if one discriminated between "amenables" and "nonamenables", the treated "amenables" did significantly better than the non-treated "amenables", whereas the "non-amenables" produced worse results after treatment.

Since this study the methods adopted for discriminating between offenders for treatment purposes have been refined. The concept of amenability has been replaced by that of inter-personal maturity, and a detailed classification has been developed. This typology has been used with some success, but there remains doubt whether the scales can be used in a reliable way in this country. The consistency in discrimination which has been achieved may have been related more to the understanding which exists between specialists operating together over a long time than to any objective standards which would ensure repeatability.

Meanwhile other scales, with greater reliability, have been developed to provide measures of anxiety, neuroticism, introversion–extraversion, and other aspects of personality. These must be tested to discover whether they can provide useful tools for dividing offenders into groups amenable to different methods of treatment. It is also to be desired that as classification develops the judgements of clinicians can have a proper place, but this places an onus on clinicians to instil some kind of discipline into their judgements to make them objectively communicable and repeatable.

Another approach still in its infancy depends on measuring the physiological differences which underlie the differences of personality and attitude which are at present being investigated. The possibility is that we may develop physiological measures of speed of conditioning, of responses in anxiety situations reflected by changes in the autonomic nervous system, which are in tune with what we have been trying to measure in other ways but which may be more reliable. Also largely unexplored is the possibility of using an analysis of roles in the inmate sub-culture of the institution as a diagnostic tool.

On the whole those in charge of offenders' training are not the best judges of future response; but in future, as there develops a more explicit differentiation of training techniques, it is feasible that those in charge of the new techniques may be able to select operationally those most suitable for each type of treatment.

Finally, it is necessary to recognize that offender classifications can only be as sophisticated as the available forms of treatment allow. The need is now to establish explicitly different forms of treatment and training. A variety of different types of regime is beginning to emerge, and there are various and different attempts at providing treatment within the training community. New methods of reintroducing the offender into the community are being tried—home leave, discharge courses, hostel schemes, after-care, and now parole. The problem is to make use of these variables systematically so that their effects can be assessed. We need an investigation of the relationship between offender and treatment variables within institutions, of a similar type to that being pursued by the Home Office Research Unit in its investigation of probation treatment (*see* p.79).

Research into classification has its own special problems. Where, as in California, research into treatment is given a priority over other classification needs, random samples can be used and a relatively simple research design can be maintained. More complicated provisions for dealing with varying needs in the system at the same time as research will almost certainly call for more complicated methodology. For example, random assignment of cases may be impossible because of pressing security or treatment priorities. One solution under consideration by prison psychologists together with members of the Home Office Research Unit is the establishment of quota groups, so that each group has its own degree of priority in relation to a given treatment variable. Other problems arise when the needs of research clash with an established treatment programme for selected offenders or when research results are used before their value has been fully assessed. Prediction tables should not be blamed for failing to make discriminations in relation to classification which they were not designed to make.

13. TREATMENT

In his paper on "The Treatment of Young Offenders", Dr. Derek Miller (XIX) limits discussion to male adolescents. Two questions are posed—"What is adolescence about?" and "What makes the adolescent behave in an anti-social way?" To answer these questions Dr. Miller suggests that adolescence can be divided into three stages. The first, the early phase of puberty covers those aged 11–12 to 13–14. At this stage the main concern is with physical changes, and behaviour is typified by gangs, groups and separation from families. This last feature makes it impossible for the same worker to work with both the adolescent and the family, although work with the family may still be necessary. The delinquent, separating himself from his family, cannot gain his accustomed support from the extended family and is liable to feel that the worker is colluding with his parents against him unless he has the exclusive attention of his worker. At this early stage of adolescence institutional treatment should only be necessary if the boy comes from a pathological family or is grossly disturbed himself.

The second period of adolescence is seen as a time of identification when the boy needs satisfactory models from people and from his social environment. Institutions for this age group are normally aberrant, totally unrelated to society at large, both in their own organization and in the models of manhood they present.

The third phase covers those aged 16–17. During this phase the more disturbed the individual and his environment, the greater is the need to keep him in a constant environment during this time. The more divisions there have been in school environment, for example, the more difficult it is for the individual to relate at any one stage.

The aetiology of delinquent behaviour in adolescence can be seen in the environment, the family and the individual, and precise diagnosis is necessary if the worker is to concentrate rather than dissipate his effort and avoid the danger of fitting the individual into the worker's own theories.

Dr. Miller describes how these views on adolescent delinquency lie behind the treatment given at the Hertfordshire Training School. This approved school tries to make its boys feel like men by basing itself on the idea that a successful man does a job successfully. The aims of the school are to train, and to train to work. In a follow-up study in 1962 it had been shown that those who chose a compatible job had a better chance of avoiding recidivism. A study in 1966 showed that on leaving the school 55 per cent of the boys had a compatible job, and that 6 months later 45 per cent still had compatible jobs. The school aims to make boys feel that their jobs are real. They are paid overtime rates and bonuses for piecework, and most of them feel that the jobs done and the people they work with are valuable. They take a pride in working well and the staff provide realistic models—they come mainly from the same social group as the boys, and are for the most part men with families, seen as sexually successful. The living arrangements ensure that the boys are not forced into dependent parental relationships.

The demand for psychiatric help for the boys far exceeds what is available. (This is perhaps a good example of the point made earlier (p. 123) that a classification system cannot be more sophisticated than the system it serves.) The only way to meet this demand is to make the environment itself therapeutic. Often it is found that the boy apparently conforming to the environment is the one most in need of help. A recent study, still unpublished, has shown that the staff are remarkably accurate in their predictions of the way boys will adapt to society and of their chances of future criminality. Dr. Miller believes that the project has been successful in creating an environment which is not aberrant, and which produces boys who know how to survive in society. Ideally, perhaps, treatment at the school should be longer and should start earlier than 16, but the school does have a hostel so that some of the boys can continue their therapy and their links with the school after leaving.

An approved school may be able to define its aims with some clarity, but in his paper on "Prisons" Mr. Alan Bainton (II) points out that the purpose of prisons is confused. The prison system mirrors the conflicts which exist within society. Society has developed a greater understanding of the difficulties facing individuals in modern urban life, so that there is a more sympathetic approach to the offender; but at the same time the decay of the formerly strong supportive influences in society have led to an increase in crime. This has heightened the essential ambivalence which society shows to offenders. Treatment and punishment are not invariably incompatible, but the combination presents great problems. Where a need for treatment can be clearly established and the means exist, as, for example, when there is evidence of a mental condition likely to respond to treatment, the course is clearly indicated. But for the greater part we follow a course of awarding penalties of increasing severity as each in turn fails, only interrupting the process when it becomes obviously inappropriate.

For those who have been dealt with in society, or by other forms of custodial treatment, the ultimate sanction is prison. There is every reason why the use of this sanction should be delayed, but considerations other than the treatment of the offender will often dictate otherwise. The seriousness of the offence, the need to deter others, and the need to protect the public, cannot be ignored. Prisons will therefore continue to exist, but with a purpose which is at present confused both by society's conflicting demands and by the numbers which over-crowd our out-of-date buildings.

The prisoner's ability to avoid any meaningful participation in training programmes is both a reflection of the prison sub-culture and a result of the system which secures his automatic release by efflux of time. If training and treatment are to have their full effect it will be necessary to introduce an element of indeterminacy, establish adequate diagnostic services, and particularize and validate forms of treatment; and since treatment in a restricted environment cannot be complete it will be necessary to provide supportive services on discharge.

Mr. David Collett (VIII) begins his paper on "The Community and After-Care" by reviewing the present provisions for helping discharged prisoners. The statutory responsibility for providing help rests on the probation and after-care service, but organized community effort in this field is growing, supplementing the work of the statutory service. Problems of delinquency in general, and after-care in particular, cannot be left to a professional service; community action and community involvement is a necessary ingredient of a satisfactory provision.

There are a number of reasons for this. To begin with, the rehabilitation of the prisoner is more likely if the community is not hostile. Then the government's penal policies have involved breaking down more and more the rigid division between total confinement and total freedom. The introduction of open prisons, home leave, outside working parties and hostel schemes, and the announced intention to establish a parole system, all to some extent presuppose a community which knows the facts about delinquency and wishes to be constructive—or at least the eventual acceptance of such schemes and their success depends on the existence of helpful community attitudes. As taxpayers, members of the public will require the use of professional social workers to be kept under scrutiny, and will expect voluntary workers to be used where there is no need for the time and skill of a paid probation officer. Finally, the community itself, if it claims to be Christian, or democratic, or civilized, will need to love its neighbour and care about its misfits.

At present the community is not well informed, and community action is inadequate in scale and quality. The first need, therefore, is for a programme of massive, deliberate, public education. This would have two aims. It would educate the public at large about delinquents, creating a better-informed, if mainly passive, population; and it would enthuse a minority of activists to function as volunteers working with the probation service. This programme should make use of all possible media, and attempt to replace or moderate the erroneous public stereotype of the ex-prisoner as a vicious thug or murderer. It would demonstrate to the public the variety of persons who come out of our prisons, indicating how many are incompetent or inadequate rather than clever or brutal.

The second important step needed is to make intelligent use of volunteers. They should be put into the front line, so that the professional social worker regards his role as selecting /training /guiding / servicing the volunteers. This gives added significance to the establishment of proper facilities for selecting and training voluntary workers. Voluntary workers can be used both to offer practical help in meeting after-care problems (e.g. the services offered by the W.R.V.S.) and to offer friendship on an individual basis, attempting to assist the ex-prisoner through a growing relationship. We need to consider further the potential of the latter role, which could be used in fields other than after-care. The use of the increasing number of well educated potential volunteers also needs consideration.

Clearly much thinking remains to be done before we can integrate the work of professional and voluntary workers in an adequate after-care service. There is no division in logic between the work of probation officers with discharged offenders and their work with those who have not been to an institution, so that such developments in community involvement can scarcely be confined to after-care. The prospect is referred to when Morrison (p. 98) speaks of constructing "some meaningful counterpart or analogue of the institutional therapeutic community in the outside community itself".

APPENDIX A

PROGRAMME

British Congress on Crime, University College, London
5–9 September 1966

Committee of Honour
Sir George Benson
Professor Francis Camps
Rt. Hon. Lord Chorley
Sir Charles Cunningham,
  K.B.E., C.B., C.V.O.
Professor Sir David Henderson
Hon. Lord Kilbrandon
Professor Sir Aubrey Lewis
Dr. H. Mannheim, O.B.E., elected Hon.
  President *in absentia.*
Professor Leon Radzinowicz, elected
  President.
Sir Joseph Simpson, K.B.E.
Professor Keith Simpson
Baroness Wootton
Rt. Hon. K. G. Younger

Planning Committee
Chairman:
Hugh J. Klare
Members:
Mrs. Anne Allen
Dr. Robert G. Andry
Dr. T. C. N. Gibbens
F. H. McClintock
Dr. Nigel Walker
J. E. Hall Williams
Observers:
R. L. Morrison
(Institute of Criminology, Cambridge)
A. T. F. Ogilvie (Scottish office)
H. B. Wilson (Home Office)

Monday, 5 September

10.15–12.30

PLENARY SESSION
OPENING ADDRESSES

Chairman:
Rt. Hon. KENNETH YOUNGER, Chairman, Howard League for
Penal Reform

10.15	INTRODUCTORY REMARKS
10.30	Rt. Hon. LORD STONHAM, Under-Secretary of State, Home Office
11.00	Dr. EDWARD GALWAY, Social Defence Section, United Nations
11.15	Mr. NORMAN BISHOP, Division of Crime Problems, Council of Europe
11.30	Dr. GEORGES FULLY, General Secretary, International Society of Criminology
11.45	Mr. HUGH J. KLARE, Secretary, Howard League for Penal Reform; Chairman, Planning Committee

2.30–4.00   GROUP LECTURES AND DISCUSSIONS
                        THEME I—CRIME AND NEW DEVELOPMENTS IN
                                    SOCIAL CONTROL

4.00–4.30   TEA

4.45–6.15   PLENARY SESSION
                        KEYNOTE   LECTURE   I—THEORIES   OF
                                    DELINQUENCY

Chairman:
Sir CHARLES CUNNINGHAM, K.C.B., formerly Permanent Under-
Secretary of State, Home Office.

Speaker:
Dr. NIGEL WALKER, Reader in Criminology, University of Oxford.

2.30–4.00   GROUP LECTURES AND DISCUSSIONS
                        THEME I—CRIME AND NEW DEVELOPMENTS IN
                                    SOCIAL CONTROL

Subject 1   **Police and Human Relations**
             Chairman: Mrs. V. CREECH JONES, J.P.
             Rapporteur: Mr. D. A. THOMAS. *Speaker.* Mr. B. N. BEBBINGTON.
Subject 2   **Police and New Techniques in Crime Control**
             Chairman: Mr. ALEC SAMUELS.
             Rapporteur: Mr. A. G. MCDONALD. *Speaker:* Mr. H. A. SARGEAUNT.
Subject 3   **Probation—Techniques and Results**
             Chairman: Mr. W. C. Todd.
             Rapporteur: Mr. M. J. DAY. *Speaker:* Dr. STEVEN FOLKARD.
Subject 4   **The Community and Aftercare**
             Chairman: Mr. FRANK DAWTRY.
             Rapporteur: Mr. A. G. M. CHRISTOPHER. *Speaker:* Mr. DAVID
             COLLETT.
Subject 5   **The Future of Classification**
             Chairman: Dr. PETER SCOTT.
             Rapporteur: Dr. MARTIN MITCHESON. *Speaker:* Mr. VERNON
             HOLLOWAY.
Subject 6   **New Concepts in the Treatment of Young Offenders**
             Chairman: Mr. L. T. HARDING.
             Rapporteur: Mrs. JENNY KENRICK. *Speaker:* Dr. DEREK MILLER.
Subject 7   **The Place of Prison in a Modern Penal System**
             Chairman: Mr. F. G. CASTELL.
             Rapporteur: Dr. N. JEPSON. *Speaker:* Mr. ALAN BAINTON.
Subject 8   **Sentencing—New Issues and Techniques**
             Chairman: Professor J. C. SMITH.
             Rapporteur: Mrs. D. WINTON. *Speaker:* Mr. E. HALL WILLIAMS.
Subject 9   **Deprived Children and Their Families**
             Chairman: Mrs. BEA SEROTA.
             Rapporteur: Mrs. D. L. HOWARD. *Speaker:* Dr. H. R. SCHAFFER.
Subject 10   **Local Authorities and Preventive Work**
             Chairman: Mr. S. R. J. TERRY.
             Rapporteur: Mr. DAVID HAXBY. *Speaker:* Miss JOAN COOPER.

Tuesday 6 September

10.00–11.00
PLENARY SESSION
REPORT AND DISCUSSION ON THEME I—CRIME AND NEW DEVELOPMENTS IN SOCIAL CONTROL

General Rapporteur: Dr. W. H. HAMMOND
Rapporteurs of Subjects 1–5.

11.00–11.30   COFFEE

11.30–12.30   PLENARY SESSION
REPORT AND DISCUSSION ON THEME I—CRIME AND NEW DEVELOPMENTS IN SOCIAL CONTROL
(*Rapporteurs* of Subjects 6–10)

12.30–2.30   LUNCH

2.30–4.00   GROUP LECTURES AND DISCUSSIONS
THEME II—CRIME AND PERSONALITY

4.00–4.30   TEA

4.45–6.15   PLENARY SESSION
KEYNOTE LECTURE II—RESEARCH AND RE-SEARCH METHODS

Chairman:
Professor LEON RADZINOWICZ, Director, Institute of Criminology, Cambridge.

Speaker:
Mr. T. S. LODGE, Director, Home Office Research Unit.

2.30–4.00   GROUP LECTURES AND DISCUSSIONS
THEME II—CRIME AND PERSONALITY

Subject 1   **Personality and Addiction**
Chairman: Dr. M. M. GLATT.
Rapporteur: Mr. R. S. TAYLOR. *Speaker:* Dr. GRIFFITH EDWARDS.

Subject 2   **The Violent Sex Offender**
Chairman: Dr. W. LINDESAY NEUSTATTER.
Rapporteur: Mr. J. L. CORDON. *Speaker:* Dr. R. P. BRITTAIN.

Subject 3   **The Recidivist and Mental Illness**
Chairman: Dr. W. GRAY.
Rapporteur: Dr. H. R. ROLLIN. *Speaker:* Dr. DONALD WEST.

Subject 4   *Cancelled*

Subject 5   **The White Collar Criminal**
Chairman: Professor O. M. MCGREGOR.
Rapporteur: Mr. ERIC STOCKDALE. *Speaker:* Dr. LOUIS BLOM-COOPER.

Subject 6   **Delinquent Teenage Types**
Chairman: Dr. P. H. CONNELL.
Rapporteur: Mr. GEOFFREY NORMAN. *Speaker:* Dr. K. R. H. WARDROP.

Subject 7 **The Motoring Offender**
 Chairman: Dr. JOHN MARTIN.
 Rapporteur: Mrs. E. GIBSON. *Speaker:* Dr. T. C. WILLETT.
Subject 8 **The Neurotic Offender**
 Chairman: Dr. ANTHONY STORR.
 Rapporteur: Mr. PAUL DE BERKER. *Speaker:* Dr. A. HYATT WILLIAMS.
Subject 9 **Psychological Studies of Approved School Boys**
 Chairman: Dr. R. G. Andry.
 Rapporteur: Mrs. BARBARA STARKEY. *Speakers:* Miss JOY MOTT and
 Miss ELIZABETH FIELD.
Subject 10 **Delinquency and the Transition from School to Work**
 Chairman: Mrs. E. DELL.
 Rapporteur: Mrs. WELLDON. *Speaker:* Dr. M. E. M. HERFORD.

Wednesday 7 September

VISITS TO H.M. PRISONS

(All visits are classified numerically and the number of visitors in each group is bracketed)
BRIXTON, Jebb Avenue, London, S.W.2.
(remand prison; stars serving less than 3 months; non-criminal prisoners)
No. 1: Prison (12). No. 2: Principal Psychologist (4)   2.30 p.m. (both)
GRENDON, Grendon Underwood, Aylesbury, Bucks.
(psychiatric centre)
No. 3: Prison (12)   2.00 p.m.
HILL HALL, Theydon Mount, Epping, Essex.
(open prison for women with short sentences)
No. 4: Prison (10)   10.00 a.m.
HOLLOWAY, Parkhurst Road, London, N.7.
(prison for women and girls; borstal; psychiatric centre)
No. 5: Prison (12). No. 6: Wing for Adolescent Girls (12)   2.00 p.m. (both)
MAIDSTONE, County Road, Maidstone, Kent.
(stars with medium and long sentences)
No. 7: Prison (12)   2.00 p.m.
PENTONVILLE, Caledonian Road, London, N.7.
(convicted prisoners awaiting sentence; ordinaries; pre-release hostel)
No. 8: Prison (12)   2.00 p.m.
WANDSWORTH, Heathfield Road, London, S.W.18.
(ordinaries; pre-release hostel)
No. 9: Prison (12). No. 10: Principal Psychologist (4).   2.30 p.m. (both)
No. 11: Recidivists Anonymous (6)   5.30 p.m.
WORMWOOD SCRUBS, Du Cane Road, London, W.12.
(stars; young prisoners serving sentences of 6 months or more; or less than 3 months, awaiting transfer; surgical and psychiatric centre; borstal; pre-release hostel)
No. 14: Psychiatric Unit (4)   10.00 a.m. (all)

VISITS TO H.M. BORSTAL INSTITUTIONS AND DETENTION CENTRES

BULLWOOD HALL, High Road, Hockley, Essex.
(closed borstal for girls; reception and allocation centre)
No. 15: Borstal (12)   2.00 p.m.
EAST SUTTON PARK, Sutton Valence, Maidstone, Kent.
(open borstal for girls)
No. 16: Borstal (12)   2.00 p.m.
FELTHAM, Bedfont Road, Feltham, Middlesex.
(closed borstal for boys)
No. 17: Borstal (12)   2.15 p.m.
FINNAMORE WOOD CAMP, near Feltham, Middlesex.
(open borstal; satellite of Feltham closed borstal)
No. 18: Borstal (10)   2.15 p.m.
AYLESBURY, Bierton Road, Aylesbury, Bucks.
(closed detention centre for senior boys)
No. 19: Detention Centre (10)   2.15 p.m.
LATCHMERE HOUSE, Church Road, Ham Common, Richmond, Surrey.
(closed detention centre for senior boys)
No. 20: Detention Centre (12)   2.30 p.m.

VISITS TO REMAND CENTRE AND REMAND HOMES

REMAND CENTRE, Woodthorpe Road, Ashford, Middlesex.
No. 21: Remand Centre (12)   2.00 p.m.
CUMBERLOW LODGE, Chalfont Road, London, S.E.25.
No. 2: Remand Home for Girls (20)   2.30 p.m.
STAMFORD HOUSE, 23 Cathnor Road, London, W.12.
No. 23: Remand Home and Classifying Centre (20)   10.30 a.m.

VISITS TO APPROVED SCHOOLS

DUNCROFT SCHOOL, Moor Lane, Staines, Middlesex.
No. 24: Approved School providing regular Psychiatric Treatment for Senior Girls for which the N.A.M.H. acts as Trustee for the Home Office; Pre-release Hostel (12)   10.30 a.m.
ROYAL PHILANTHROPIC SOCIETY'S SCHOOL, Redhill, Surrey.
No. 25: Approved School Boys' Classifying School; Senior Boys' Training School; Special Closed Unit (10)   11.00 a.m.

VISITS TO CLINICS, INSTITUTES, etc.

BORSTAL AFTERCARE ASSOCIATION, 2 Abbey Gardens, Great College Street, London, S.W.1.
No. 26: Offices of the Association (10)   10.30 a.m.
HENDERSON HOSPITAL, Brighton Road, Sutton, Surrey.
(psychiatric treatment of delinquents in a therapeutic community)
No. 27: Seminar on Work of Hospital (20)   2.15 p.m.
HOME OFFICE RESEARCH UNIT, Horseferry House, Thorney Street, London, S.W.1.
No. 28: Work of the Unit (20)   3.00 p.m.

K

HOWARD LEAGUE FOR PENAL REFORM, 6 Endsleigh Street,
London, W.C.1.
No. 29: Work of the League (6)   3.00 p.m.
INNER LONDON PROBATION AND AFTERCARE SERVICE,
1a Walton Street, London, S.W.3.
No. 30: Work of the Service (6)   11.00 p.m.
INSTITUTE OF PSYCHIATRY, Maudsley Hospital, Denmark
Hill, London, S.W.5.
No. 31: Work of the Institute (6)   10.00 a.m.
INSTITUTE FOR THE STUDY AND TREATMENT OF DELINQUENCY,
8 Bourdon Street, Davies Street, London, W.1.
No. 32: Work of the Institute (6)   3.00 p.m.
JAZZ CLUB ON EEL PIE ISLAND, Twickenham, Middlesex.
(club run by a detached worker)
No. 33: The Club (6)   9.00 p.m.
No. 34: The Club (6)   10.00 p.m.
PORTMAN CLINIC, 8 Bourdon Street, Davies Street, London,
W.1.
No. 35: The Clinic (6)   3.00 p.m.
ST. BERNARD'S HOSPITAL, Southall, Middlesex.
No. 36: Regional Alcoholic and Addiction Unit (6)   10.30 a.m.
TAVISTOCK CLINIC, 56 Hallam Street, London, W.1.
No. 37: Adolescent Unit (6)   3.00 p.m.
TOOTING BEC HOSPITAL, Tooting Bec Road, London,
S.W.17.
No. 38: Unit for the Treatment of Alcoholics (6)   2.30 p.m.

Thursday 8 September

10.00–11.00   PLENARY SESSION

REPORT AND DISCUSSION ON THEME II—CRIME AND PERSONALITY

General Rapporteur: Mr. DOUGLAS GIBSON
Rapporteurs of Subjects 1–5.

11.00–11.30   COFFEE

11.30–12.30   PLENARY SESSION

REPORT AND DISCUSSION ON THEME II—CRIME AND PERSONALITY

Rapporteurs of Subjects 6–10

12.30–2.30   LUNCH

2.30–4.00   GROUP LECTURES AND DISCUSSIONS

THEME III—CRIME AND SOCIETY

(for details see opposite page)

4.00–4.30   TEA

4.45–6.15   PLENARY SESSION

KEYNOTE LECTURE III—PREVENTION AND TREATMENT

Chairman:
Hon. Lord KILBRANDON, Judge of the Scottish High Court.

Speaker:
Mr. R. L. MORRISON, Deputy Director, Institute of Criminology, Cambridge.

2.30–4.00   GROUP LECTURES AND DISCUSSIONS

THEME III—CRIME AND SOCIETY

Subject 1 **Drug-Takers and their Social Setting**
Chairman: Dr. CEDRIC WILSON.
Rapporteur: Dr. ARNOLD LINKEN. *Speaker:* Mr. A. CHISNALL.

Subject 2 **Sex Deviance and Community Attitudes**
Chairman: Dr. W. J. BOLT.
Rapporteur: Mrs. JEANNE TAYLOR. *Speaker:* Mr. MICHAEL SCHOFIELD.

Subject 3 **Illness in Parents and Delinquency in the Children**
Chairman: Professor FRANCIS CAMPS.
Rapporteur: Mr. J. F. SMITH. *Speaker:* Dr. MICHAEL RUTTER.

Subject 4 **Company Fraud**
Chairman: Mr. AMBROSE APPELBE.
Rapporteur: Mr. A. SIMPSON. *Speaker:* Mr. MORRIS FINER, Q.C.

Subject 5 **Vagrancy**
Chairman: Mrs. ANNE ALLEN.
Rapporteur: Mrs. DOUGLAS GIBSON. *Speaker:* Mr. A. WALLICH-CLIFFORD.

Subject 6 **Delinquency amongst Immigrants**
Chairman: Professor JOHN MAYS.
Rapporteur: Mr. D. M. LOWSON. *Speaker:* Mr. A. E. BOTTOMS.

Subject 7 **Adolescence and Delinquency**
Chairman: Professor FRANCOIS LAFITTE.
Rapporteur: Mr. CHRISTOPHER HOLTOM. *Speaker:* Dr. H. M. HOLDEN.

Subject 8 **Crime Prevention in Schools**
Chairman: Dr. E. SIMPSON.
Rapporteur: Mrs. B. J. KAHAN. *Speaker:* Mr. J. McNALLY.

Subject 9 **Status Frustration and Delinquency**
Chairman: Mr. D. L. HOWARD.
Rapporteur: Mrs. PAULINE MORRIS. *Speaker:* Mr. S. COHEN (on behalf of Dr. DAVID DOWNES)

Subject 10 **Changing Patterns of Criminal Behaviour**
Chairman: Dr. CHARLOTTE BANKS.
Rapporteur: Mr. S. KLEIN. *Speaker:* Mr. N. HOWARD AVISON.

Friday 9 September

10.00–11.00   PLENARY SESSION
REPORT AND DISCUSSION ON THEME III—CRIME AND SOCIETY
General Rapporteurs: Mr. F. E. McCLINTOCK
Rapporteurs of Subjects 1–5.

11.00–11.30   COFFEE
11.30–12.30   PLENARY SESSION
REPORT AND DISCUSSION ON THEME III—CRIME AND SOCIETY
Rapporteurs of Subjects 6–10

12.30   PLENARY SESSION
CLOSING ADDRESS
Speaker: Dr. T. C. N. GIBBENS.

APPENDIX B

LECTURERS

The numbers opposite speakers' names are those that are used in the text.
IR opposite a speaker's name denotes introductory remarks.
C opposite a speaker's name denotes concluding remarks.
N = No written summary was received.
OA = Opening Address.

I   N. HOWARD AVISON, Lecturer in Criminology, University of Edinburgh.

II   ALAN BAINTON, Assistant Director, Prison Department.

III   B. N. BEBBINGTON, Director, Police Research and Planning Branch, Home Office.

IR   NORMAN BISHOP, Head, Division of Crime Problems, Council of Europe.

IV   Dr. LOUIS BLOM-COOPER, Barrister, Director of Institute of Sociology of Law, Bedford College.

V   A. E. BOTTOMS, Institute of Criminology, Cambridge University.

N   Dr. R. P. BRITTAIN, Consultant Psychiatrist, State Hospital, Carstairs Junction, Lanark.

VI   ARTHUR CHISNALL, Detached social worker, Twickenham, Middlesex.

VII   STANLEY COHEN, Lecturer in Sociology, Enfield College of Technology, London.

VIII   DAVID COLLETT, Director, London Federation of Community Centres.

IX   JOAN COOPER, Chief Inspector, Home Office Children's Department.

X   Dr. GRIFFITH EDWARDS, Consultant Psychiatrist, Maudsley Hospital.

XI   ELIZABETH FIELD, Home Office Research Unit.

XII   MORRIS FINER, Q.C., Barrister.

XIII   Dr. Steven Folkard, Home Office Research Unit, i/c probation research projects.

IR   Dr. GEORGES FULLY, General Secretary, International Society of Criminology, Paris.

IR   Dr. EDWARD GALWAY, Adviser on Social Defence, United Nations, Geneva.

C   Dr. T. C. N. GIBBENS, Reader in Forensic Psychiatry, Institute of Psychiatry, Maudsley Hospital.

XIV   Dr. M. E. M. HERFORD, Appointed Factory Doctor, Windsor and Slough District.

XV   Dr. H. M. HOLDEN, Consultant Psychiatrist, Tavistock Clinic.

XVI   VERNON HOLLOWAY, Principal Psychologist, Prison Service, London.

IRC   HUGH J. KLARE, Secretary Howard League for Penal Reform; Chairman Planning Committee of the British Congress on Crime.

XVII   T. S. LODGE, Director, Home Office Research Unit.

137

XVIII   J. McNALLY, National Foundation for Educational Research.

XIX   Dr. DEREK H. MILLER, Consultant Psychiatrist, Adolescent Unit, Tavistock Clinic.

XX   R. L. MORRISON, Deputy Director, Institute of Criminology, Cambridge.

XXI   JOY W. MOTT, Home Office Research Unit.

XXII   Dr. MICHAEL RUTTER, Consultant Psychiatrist.

XXIII   H. A. SARGEAUNT, Chief Scientific Adviser, Home Office.

XXIV   Dr. H. R. SCHAFFER, Senior Lecturer in Psychology, University of Strathclyde.

XXV   MICHAEL SCHOFIELD, Psychologist.

OA   Rt. Hon. LORD STONHAM, O.B.E., Parliamentary Under-Secretary of State, Home Office.

XXVI   Dr. NIGEL WALKER, Reader in Criminology and Fellow of Nuffield College, Oxford University.

N   A. WALLICH-CLIFFORD, Social Worker, Simon Community Trust.

XXVII   Dr. K. R. H. WARDROP, Director, Forensic Psychiatric Clinic, Glasgow.

XXVIII   Dr. DONALD WEST, Psychiatrist, Assistant Director, Institute of Criminology, Cambridge University.

XXIX   Dr. T. C. WILLETT, Dept. of Sociology, University of Reading.

XXX   ERYL HALL WILLIAMS, Reader in Criminology, London School of Economics.

XXXI   Dr. A. HYATT WILLIAMS, Consultant Psychiatrist, Tavistock Clinic.

IRC   Rt. Hon. KENNETH G. YOUNGER, Chairman, Home Office Advisory Council on the Treatment of Offenders; Chairman, Howard League for Penal Reform.

APPENDIX C
BRITISH CONGRESS ON CRIME

LIST OF PARTICIPANTS (excluding lecturers)

L. J. ACKROYD, Home Office, Dangerous Drugs Branch.
F. AINSWORTH, H.M. Borstal Service.
JAMES AITON, County Convenor, Hamilton.
SIMON ALBURY.
ERIC ALEXANDER, Teacher, Holland.
Mrs. MIEK ALEXANDER, Sociologist. Holland.
Mrs. ANNE ALLEN, Journalist.
Miss CHARLOTTE ALLEN, Student.
J. P. D. ALLEN, Principal Probation Officer.
Mrs. P. ALLEN, Social Worker, Wormwood Scrubs.
Mr. AMPONSAH, Ghana, Voluntary Social Worker, South West London.
J. J. M. ANDERSON, Assistant Governor.
Mrs. R. V. ANDREWS, J.P., Secretary, Case Conference.
Dr. ROBERT ANDRY, Lecturer in Psychology, London University.
Mrs. H. S. ANTHONY, Home Office Research Unit.
AMBROSE APPELBE, Solicitor.
Mrs. MARGARET ARCHER.
C. F. ASCHER, Lawyer.
J. M. ATKINSON, Home Office Research Unit.
G. B. AVES, Southampton Probation Service.

C. S. BAGSHAW, Southampton Probation Service.
Miss F. H. BAKER, Home Office Research Unit.
Dr. CHARLOTTE BANKS, Lecturer in Psychology, University of London.
A. BANNERMAN, Principal Probation Officer, Leeds.

JOHN BARBOUR, Probation Officer, Dumfries.
Miss ALISON BARNARD.
Det. Supt. BARNETT, Metropolitan Police.
Miss DEIDRA BEACHAM, Student.
Miss A. BECKER, Secretary, Friends Penal Affairs Committee.
Chief Supt. BECKE, Metropolitan Police.
R. H. BEESON, O.B.E., Senior Inspector, Probation and After-Care Department, Home Office.
M. BELLAMY, Student.
Det. Chief Supt. BELLAMY, Research and Planning Branch, New Scotland Yard.
B. J. BENNETT, Scottish Education Department.
Prof. A. BERISTAIN, S.J., Professor of Criminal Law, University of Bilbao.
G. BEVIS, Devon and Exeter Probation Service.
Dr. ROBERT BLAIR, Psychiatrist.
Miss S. Z. BLATCH, Southampton Probation Service.
Mrs. DAPHNE BLEACH, Children's Department, London Borough of Hackney.
Mrs. BLOOMAN, Middlesex Probation Service.
Miss L. K. BLOOR, Home Office Research Unit.
Dr. ROBERT BLUGLASS, Physician, Royal Dundee Liff Hospital.
Dr. K. W. BLYTH, Nuffield Foundation.
Rev. Dr. W. J. BOLT, Howard League for Penal Reform.
Mrs. E. F. BOND, Ashford Remand Centre.

139

A. K. Bottomley, Student.
Rev. Neville Boundy.
J. D. Bradbury, Southampton Probation Service.
Miss Rose M. Braithwaite, Lecturer in Case Work, Bedford College.
Miss Joan Branton, Psychologist, Winston Green Prison.
A. J. E. Brennan, Asst. Secretary, Criminal Department, Home Office.
Dr. Lisbeth Briess, Psychologist.
Miss K. M. Brown, Probation Officer, Balham Magistrates Court.
R. C. Brown, Children's Department, London Borough of Hackney.
Philip Burgess, Student.
J. L. Burns, Principal, Kingswood Approved and Classifying Schools.
James E. Burrow, Principal Probation Officer, Dumbarton.

Sir Ralph Campbell, Supreme Court, Nassau, Bahamas.
Prof. F. Camps, Forensic Medicine, London Hospital.
M. B. Carey,
W. K. Carlton,
Miss M. M. Carver, Home Office Research Unit.
F. G. Castell, General Secretary, Prison Officers Association.
Dr. W. E. Cavenagh, j.p., Lecturer, University of Birmingham.
Jonathan Chadwick, Student.
Miss M. D. Chorlton.
H. B. Christian, Dental Officer, Prison Service.
J. B. W. Christie, Sheriff Substitute, Dundee.
Supt. Christie, Metropolitan Police.
Anthony Christopher, Chairman, Royal London Discharged Prisoners Aid Society.
K. W. Clark.
Robin Clark, Student.
R. V. G. Clarke, Research Worker, Kingswood Classifying School.
John Coker, Assistant Principal Probation Officer, Hampshire.
Miss Janis Cooper,
Dr. P. H. Connell, Consultant Psychiatrist, Maudsley Hospital.

A. E. Corben, Criminal Department, Home Office.
J. L. Cordon, Middlesex Probation Service.
Miss E. P. Corner, Probation and After-care Department, Home Office.
D. J. Cowperthwaite, Assistant Secretary, Scottish Home and Health Department.
Dr. H. B. Craigie, Scottish Home and Health Department.
W. H. Craike, Royal Philanthropic School.
I.J.Croft, Home Office Research Unit.
B. C. Cubbon, Criminal Department, Home Office.
Sir Charles Cunningham, k.c.b., Deputy Chairman, U.K. Atomic Energy Authority; formerly Permanent Under-Secretary, Home Office.
H. A. Currell.

Sheriff L. Daiches, Glasgow.
Miss Mary Dargie, Probation Officer, Ayr.
Clive Davies, Sociologist and Barrister.
J. Davies, Southend-on-Sea Probation Service.
M. B. Davies, Home Office Research Unit.
Det. Chief Inspector Davis, Metropolitan Police.
R. H. Davis, Chief Officer, H.M.B. Hewell Grange.
Frank Dawtry, m.b.e., General Secretary, National Association of Probation Officers.
Michael Day, Senior Probation Officer, West Sussex.
N. D. Deakin, Institute of Race Relations.
Frederick Dean, Manager, Sedbury Park School.
Miss Grace Dean.
Miss P. C. R. Deane, Inner London Probation Service.
Paul de Berker, Principal Psychologist, Prison Service.
Mrs. de Laszlo.
Mrs. S. Dell.
J. H. Dickinson, Principal Probation Officer, North-East London

R. W. DOWNTON, Governor, H.M. Prison, Norwich.

Miss B. E. DRAKE, Chief Officer, London Borough of Tower Hamlets.

Rev. J. H. DREW, Prison Department, Home Office.

T. H. DUFFIELD, Children's Department, Borough of Hackney.

JOHN DUNPHY, Inner London Probation and After-care Service.

E. W. J. DURAND.

Mrs. ESTHER DURAS.

Mrs. WINIFRED ELLAND.

J. T. ELLIS, No. 4 Regional Crime Squad, Birmingham.

Dr. MARY ELLIS, Medical Officer, Feltham Borstal Institution.

DUNCAN FAIRN, Assistant Under-Secretary, Home Office.

L. FARMER, Assistant Chief Constable, Wakefield.

GEORGE FENN, Police Training Centre, Harpesley Hall.

MORRIS FINER, Q.C., Barrister-at-Law.

J. H. FITCH, Principal Psychologist, Wormwood Scrubs.

Supt. FLEMING, Metropolitan Police.

Mrs. H. E. FORBES, Principal, Prison Department, Home Office.

PATRICK FORBES, Prison Visitors' Association.

Sheriff H. FORD, Angus.

ROBERT FOREN, Department of Social Sciences, Bradford.

Miss ROSEMARY FOX.

Miss JANET FRANCIS.

Miss KATHLEEN FRANCIS, Senior Youth Officer, Wandsworth.

Dr. MARJORIE FRANKLIN, Consultant Psychiatrist.

H. A. FRASER, Chief Officer, Glenogle Senior Detention Centre, Wolverhampton.

Mrs. MARGARET FRASER,

Det. Chief Supt. W. FRENCH, City of London Police.

B. J. FRISBY, Assistant Governor, Wellingborough Borstal.

J. FRISBY, Governor, Polmont Borstal.

H. M. GARLAND, Senior Probation Officer, Aberdeen.

Miss MARJORIE GAYSUNAS, Henderson Hospital.

JOHN GEORGE, Stamford House Remand Home.

Miss BARBARA GIBSON.

Mrs. DOUGLAS GIBSON, Social Worker, Circle Trust.

DOUGLAS GIBSON, Secretary, Central Council of Probation Committees.

Mrs. EVELYN GIBSON, Home Office Research Unit.

J. L. GILDER, Assistant Director, Prison Department.

Miss P. GLAISHER, Henderson Hospital.

BRYAN GLASTONBURY, Social Administration Department, University of Swansea.

Dr. M. M. GLATT, Consultant Psychiatrist, St. Bernard's Hospital, Southall.

Mrs. B. GLEAVE, University of Bath.

Miss W. M. GOODE, Probation and After-Care Department, Home Office.

Miss N. M. GOODMAN, Home Office Research Unit.

G. H. Gordon, Department of Criminal Law and Criminology, Edinburgh University.

V. G. GOTTS, Probation and After-Care Department, Home Office.

A. GOULD, Governor, Dover Borstal.

Mrs. JOAN GOULD.

J. W. GOYDER, Assistant Commissioner, City of London Police.

DAVID GRAY, Chief Constable, Police, Stirling.

Dr. WILLIAM GRAY, Medical Superintendent, Grendon Prison Hospital.

Dr. WENDY GREENGROSS, Medical Consultant, Marriage Guidance Council.

J. A. GRIEVES, Q.C., Deputy Chairman, Middlesex Sessions.

T. A. GRIFFITHS.

W. A. GRIFFITHS, Southampton Probation Service.

GEORGE GROSS.

DERMOT O'C. GRUBB, Assistant Governor, Wandsworth Prison.

E. H. GWYNN, C.B., Deputy Under-Secretary of State, Home Office.

Mr. P. HADDON.

ARTHUR HAGUE, Home Office.

Miss JEAN GRAHAM HALL, Stipendiary Magistrate.

M. HALL.

Dr. W. H. HAMMOND, Home Office Research Unit.

M. G. HANCOCK, Children's Department, London Borough of Southwark.

Dr. N. E. HAND, Police Research and Planning Branch Home Office.

R. P. HARBORD, Student.

L. T. HARDING, Principal, Herts. Training School.

F. L. HARRAP, Assistant Governor, Huntercombe Borstal.

Mrs. N. HARRIS, Children's Department, London Borough of Hackney.

BRENDON HART, Prison Officer, Brixton Prison.

Mrs. L. HARVEY.

DAVID HAXBY, Assistant Secretary, National Association of Probation Officers.

A. G. HAYDEN.

THOMAS HAYES, Assistant Director, Prison Department.

Lt.-Col. J. HAYWOOD, Assistant Director, Prison Department.

E. C. HEAD, Prison Officer, Wormwood Scrubs.

Mrs. CHRISTINA HEDDLE.

H. J. HEILBO, Prison Governor, Denmark.

Mrs. MARY HELLIER, Department of Social Sciences, Bradford Institute of Technology.

Miss CELIA HENSMAN, Institute of Psychiatry, Maudsley Hospital.

AUBREY HEWINSON.

DAVID HEWLINGS, Principal, Staff Training College, Prison Service.

D. H. HILARY, Criminal Department, Home Office.

T. HILL, Welfare Department, Brixton Prison.

Miss JENNIFER HILTON,

Miss S. A. HIMMEL, Middlesex Probation Service.

Det. Supt. HIXSON, Metropolitan Police.

Comdr. G. B. HODGKINSON, R.N.

Dr. PETER HOEFNAGELS, Sociologist, Utrecht, Holland.

Det. Supt. HOGGINS, Metropolitan Police.

G. E. HOLDEN, Assistant Secretary, Rayner Foundation.

Miss J. HOLDITCH, Southampton Probation Service.

CHRISTOPHER HOLTOM, Lecturer in Social Work, University of Bristol.

Miss M. HORNSBY, Immigration Department, Home Office.

MORRIS HOROVITCH, Headmaster, Hutton Residential School.

Miss E. M. HOUSTON, Barrister, Secretary, Scottish Branch HLPR.

B. R. HOWARD.

Mrs. ELISABETH HOWARD, Child Care Officer, Sussex Detention Centre.

D. L. HOWARD, Lecturer in Sociology, Institute of Education, Brighton.

J. A. HOWARD, Criminal Department, Home Office.

Miss J. E. C. HOYTEN, H.M.B.I., Hatfield.

Mrs. M. HUDSON.

BRIAN HUGHES, Department Extra-Mural Studies, University of Southampton.

P. E. HUGHES, Notting Hill Social Council.

Miss S. A. HUGHES, Southampton Probation Service.

Mrs. MARY ILES, Social Worker.

VICTOR JACKOPSON, Student.

S. C. JACKSON, Criminal Department, Home Office.

Miss A. G. JACOB, Southampton Probation Service.

Prof. T. E. JAMES, Kings College London (Law).

JOHN E. JENKINS, Prison Officer, Rochester Borstal.

Dr. N. JEPSON, Senior Lecturer in Criminology, University of Leeds.

Sheriff C. JOHNSTON, Q.C., Glasgow.

J. O. JOHNSTON, Scottish Home and Health Department, Edinburgh.

RONALD JONES, Children's Officer, Swansea.

Mrs. V. Creech Jones, j.p., Executive Committee HLPR.

Dr. W. Jonkers, Holland.

M. C. Joseph, Children's Department, Home Office.

Mrs. B. J. Kahan, Children's Officer, Oxford.

W. Kallwass.

D. R. Keir, Principal Probation Officer, Lanarkshire.

Supt. Kelley, Metropolitan Police.

J. C. Kelly, Inner London Probation Service.

Hugh Kenyon, Director, Prison Department.

Jenny Kenrick, Former Probation Officer.

Stuart Kermack, Sheriff Substitute, Elgin, Scotland.

Miss Rosalind Kerstein.

Lord Kilbrandon, Lord of Session, Scotland.

R. S. King, Prison Department, Home Office.

W. E. Kirkham, Assistant Superintendent of Prisons, Uganda.

S. Klein, Home Office Research Unit.

Prof. F. Lafitte, Dept. of Social Studies, University of Birmingham.

Geoffrey Lampard.

J. R. C. Lee, Prison Officer's Training School, Wakefield.

David Leigh-Hunt, Student.

L. I. Lerego, Prison Dept. Home Office.

G. E. Lewis, Hammersmith Probation Office.

Miss W. E. Lewis.

F. Liesching, Governor, Latchmere House, Detention Centre.

W. H. Lincoln, Prison Officer, Stoke Heath Borstal.

Dr. Arnold Linken, Physician, Student Health Centre, University College, London.

Miss Gillian Lincoln, Student.

Prof. M. Lopez Rey, formerly U.N. Social Defence.

David Lowson, University Settlement, Liverpool.

Mrs. Karin Lundin, Denmark.

K. M. Lyon, Home Office Research Unit.

J. Mallett, Prison Welfare Department, Oakham Prison.

Leon Mangin, Family Court Mental Health Clinic, Nassau County, U.S.A.

Mrs. B. Mann.

Gunnar Marnell, Group Director, Swedish Prison Service.

Miss M. Marston, Association of Assistant Mistresses.

Prof. J. P. Martin, University of Southampton, Department of Sociology.

Dr. K. R. Masani, Psychotherapist, Prison Service.

Miss M. May, Senior Probation Officer, Inner London.

Stanley Mayne, Inner London Education Authority.

Prof. J. B. Mays, University of Liverpool.

George Mercer, Principal Probation Officer, Stirling.

Mrs. Sybil Merrick.

W. Middelmass, Immigration Department, Home Office.

B. G. Milne, Stamford House Remand Centre.

A. A. Milnes, H.M. Prison, Brixton.

Mrs. E. Mitchell,

Dr. M. Mitcheson, Psychiatrist, Maudsley Hospital.

Miss June Montgomery, School of Social Sciences, Brunel College.

E. Moonman, m.p., House of Commons, S.W.1.

Rev. W. L. Morgan, British Council on Christian Society and the Homosexual.

Dr. J. K. W. Morrice, Consultant Psychiatrist, Dingleton Hospital, Melrose, Scotland.

Mrs. M. Morris, Middlesex Probation Service.

Mrs. Pauline Morris, Sociology Department, University of Essex.

D. A. C. Morrison, Probation and After-Care Department Home Office.

Peter Mortimer, Probation Officer, Dewsbury.

LAURENCE MOSELEY, Department of Social Administration, Swansea.

R. W. MOTT, Children's Department, Home Office.

Det. Chief Inspector MOUNSEY, Lancashire Constabulary.

Rev. JAMES K. MURREN, Sociologist.

F. H. McCLINTOCK, Assistant Director, Institute of Criminology.

A. G. McDONALD, Scientific Advisers Branch, Home Office.

Mrs. EVELYN MacDONALD, Department of Law, University of Strathclyde.

Dr. LYNN McDONALD, Professor of Criminology, Canada.

Prof. O. M. McGREGOR, Bedford College, London.

Mrs. J. MACKIE, Hon. Treasurer, Fife County Probation Committee.

Mrs. VALERIE McLEAN, Secretary, Parents Involved.

JOHN McMILLAN, Research Assistant, University of Reading.

Mrs. F. McNEILLE, Secretary, Margery Fry Memorial Fund, Birmingham Area.

JAMES McNICOL, Principal Probation Officer, Kirkaldy.

Miss BESSIE MACONACHIE, M.P., Northern Ireland.

JOHN McPHERSON, Scottish Education Department.

Dr. PAUL McQUAID, Mater Hospital, Dublin.

N. NEAVE, Governor, Edinburgh Young Offenders' Institute.

P. A. Nettleton, Middlesex Probation Service.

Dr. LINDESAY NEUSTATTER, Consultant Psychiatrist, St. Ebba's Hospital.

GEOFFREY NORMAN, Prison Welfare Officer, Manchester.

Chief Supt. NORMAN, Metropolitan Police.

C. P. NUTTALL, Home Office Research Unit.

A. P. OAKLEY, ex-Probation Officer, now Graduate Student.

M. O'CALLAGHAN, Headmaster, Rowley Hall School, Staffs.

R. T. OERTON, Solicitor.

P. P. OKETA, Superintendent Prisons, Uganda.

F. L. OKWAARE, Commissioner of Prisons, Uganda.

A. M. OKWONGA, Superintendent Prisons, Uganda.

Mrs. G. E. O'LEARY, Home Office Research Unit.

STEPHEN OLNEY, Student.

A. OWOR, Superintendent Prisons, Uganda.

M. W. PALMER, Criminal Appeal Office.

J. PANNELL, Inner London Probation Service.

J. R. PARKER, Postgraduate Student of Criminology, Cambridge University.

A. J. PEARSON, Assistant Governor, Maidstone.

DAVID PERYER.

B. J. PHILLIPS.

Miss EDNA PHILLIPS.

Dr. I. G. PICKERING, Director, Medical Service, Prison Department.

C. R. PIDDUCK, Psychology Department, Inner London Education Authority.

M. J. PIGOTT, Southampton Probation Service.

Prof. JEAN PINATEL, International Society of Criminology

T. C. PLATT, Children's Department, Home Office.

DENIS POTTS, Borstal After-Care

Dr. M. J. POWER, Social Medicine Research Unit, London.

NIGEL POWER, New York.

J. PREECE, Children and Family Advice Department, Kent.

Miss J. B. PRICE, Home Office Research Unit.

Mrs. A. M. QUIN.

Prof. AIMEE RACINE, Institute of Delinquency Studies, Brussels, Belgium.

Prof. L. RADZINOWICZ, Director, Institute of Criminology, Cambridge.

Dr. R. RATCLIFF, Scottish Home and Health Department.

S. Ratcliffe, Inner London Probation Service.

G. Rawlings, Inner London Probation Service.

Miss S. Reader, Home Office Research Unit.

Bryan Reed, N.A.C.R.O., Deputy Director.

L. A. Robertson, Children's Officer, Westminster.

L. A. J. Robins, Southampton Probation Service.

Thomas Robson, Romilly Association.

Dr. H. R. Rollin, Consultant Psychiatrist, Horton Hospital.

Lady Rothschild, J.P., Chairman, Cambridge Magistrates Court.

C. A. F. Russell, Statistical Branch, Somerset House.

Prof. M. Russell, Lair School, Trinity College, Dublin.

A. F. Rutherford, H.M. Borstal, Hewell Grange.

Mrs. E. A. Sandars, Criminal Department, Home Office.

Alec Samuels, Lecturer in Law, University of Southampton.

Miss Eve Saville, General Secretary, I.S.T.D.

Dr. Hans Schneider, Lecturer in Criminology, University of Freiburg, Federal Republic of Germany.

A. Scott, Probation Officer, Durham.

Dr. P. D. Scott, Consultant Psychiatrist, Maudsley Hospital.

Miss Diana Seabrooke.

Dr. I. M. Seglow, Psychotherapist and Psychologist.

S. G. Seisay, Sierra Leone Prison Service.

Mrs. Bea Serota, Chairman, Education Committee, Greater London Council.

Miss M. J. Shaw, Home Office Research Unit.

Michael Sheehan.

Dr. E. Shoenberg, Social Medicine Research Unit (M.R.C.).

Emmanouel Sifakis, Senior Police Inspector, City Police, Athens, Greece.

W. H. Simons, Prison Department, Home Office.

Anthony Simpson, Barrister.

Dr. Esther Simpson, Department of Education and Science, Whitehall.

I. A. Sinclair, Home Office Research Unit.

T. B. Skinner, Scottish Home and Health Department, Edinburgh.

Mrs. Rosemary Small, Howard League for Penal Reform.

Dr. Ann Smith, University of Edinburgh.

Sheriff Aikman Smith, Aberdeen.

C. L. Smith, City of Southampton Probation Service.

G. B. Smith, Assistant Director, Prison Department, Home Office.

Prof. J. C. Smith, Department of Law, Nottingham.

Jef Smith, Child Care Officer.

W. McGregor Smith, Chief Constable, Aberdeen.

James K. Sofidiya, Researcher in Criminology, University of London.

Michael Sorensen, Social Worker, Blackfriars Settlement.

H. B. Spear, Dangerous Drugs Branch, Home Office.

Miss G. M. Stafford, Probation Officer (Inner London).

Dr. Fergus Stallard, Forensic Psychiatric Clinic, Glasgow.

Mrs. Barbara Starkey, Psychiatric Social Worker.

Mrs. Marion F. Stern, J.P.

Miss J. Stevenson, Westminster Probation Office.

Bryan Steward, Ipswich Civic College.

Eric Stockdale, Barrister-at-Law.

Dr. Anthony Storr, Consultant Psychiatrist, London.

K. H. Strange.

Dr. Mavis Stratford, J.P., Magistrate and physician, London.

Andrew Stronach, Chairman, Stirling and Clackmannan Probation Service.

Miss D. I. Sullivan, Inner London Probation Service.

Miss J. P. L. Sullivan, Inner London Probation Service.

Dr. M. Sunderland, Henderson Hospital.

C. T. SWANN, Probation and After-Care Department, Home Office.
R. D. S. SWANN, Consultant on Industries, Prison Department, Home Office.

Dr. FRANK TAIT, Medical Department, Inner London Education Authority.
H. B. TAUNTON, Southampton Probation Service.
H. J. TAYLOR, Chief Director, Prison Department, Home Office.
Mrs. JEANNE TAYLOR, Probation Officer.
R. S. TAYLOR, Principal Psychologist, Wakefield Prison.
S. R. J. Terry, Children's Department, Southwark.
P. P. THAYER, Children's Department, Home Office.
W. W. THEAKER, Children's Department, Hackney.
Sir GERALD THESIGER, High Court Judge.
D. A. THOMAS, Lecturer, Law Faculty, L.S.E., London.
SPENCE FORD THOMSON, Deputy Clerk, Aberdeen Police Court.
C. A. THORNTON, Oxfordshire Probation Service.
Dr. J. J. TOBIAS, Police College.
W. C. TODD, M.B.E., Principal Probation Officer, Middlesex.
Dr. H. P. TOLLINGTON, Consultant Psychiatrist, Grendon.
R. B. TOUGH, Aberdeen Probation Service.
E. A. TOWNDROW, Governor, Blundeston Prison.
R. T. TUDOR, Statistical Branch, Home Office.
D. G. TURNER, Criminal Department, Home Office.
T. P. TURNER, Police Research and Planning Branch, Home Office.

JOHN UTTERSON, Scottish Home and Health Department.

Dr. P. van BOXTEL, Holland.
M. VASSART, Social Worker, Centre d'Étude de la Delinquance Juvenile, Brussels.

Mrs. BETTY VERNON, I.L.E.A.
N. D. VESSEY, Southampton Probation Service.
NOEL VINTER.
P. M. W. VOELCKER, Ragner Foundation, Caernarvon.

D. G. WADDILOVE, Director of Borstal Administration, Home Office.
A. J. S. WALKER, Faculty of Arts, Edinburgh University.
M. L. WALTERS, Student.
Mrs. JENNIFER WATES, J.P., Magistrate, London.
Prof. A. S. WATSON, Professor of Law and Psychology, University of Michigan.
D. WEBSTER.
Miss J. WEBSTER, Henderson Hospital.
T. G. WEILER, Assistant Secretary, Home Office.
NATHAN WEINSTOCK, Centre National de Criminologie, Brussels.
Mrs. E. WELLDON, Senior Caseworker, Family Welfare Association.
A. B. WELLS, Middlesex Probation Service.
Dr. WILLIAM WESTON, H.M. Prison, Wakefield.
J. M. WHETTON, Institute of Social and Economic Research, Kingston, Jamaica.
Mrs. MARJORIE J. WHITE,
CYRIL WHITE.
Dr. J. S. WHITELEY, Director, Henderson Hospital.
J. WHITLEY.
E. W. WHITMORE, Police College, Branshill.
JOSEPH WHITTY, Assistant Governor, Blundeston Prison.
J. WILBURG, Probation Officer, Guayana.
Miss D. WILD, Essex Probation Service.
Miss J. W. WILDMAN, Student.
P. WILES, Student.
GERRY WILLIAMS, Henderson Hospital.
Det. Supt. WILLIAMS, Metropolitan Police.
Mrs. JOYCE B. WILLIAMS, J.P., Magistrate.

N. A. P. WILLMER, Police Research and Planning Branch, Home Office.

Bailie WILLIAM WILSON, Chairman, Fife and Dunfermline Probation Committee.

Dr. CEDRIC WILSON, Professor of Pharmacology, University of Dublin.

H. B. Wilson, Assistant Under-Secretary of State, Home Office.

Dr. HARRIETT WILSON, Sociologist, University of Birmingham.

JOHN L. WILSON, Loamingdale School.

Mrs. DOROTHY WINTON, J.P., Magistrate.

Mrs. ROSEMARY WOODWARD, J.P., Magistrate.

MARTIN WRIGHT, Secretary, Institute of Criminology.

Det. Chief Inspector YATES, Metropolitan Police.